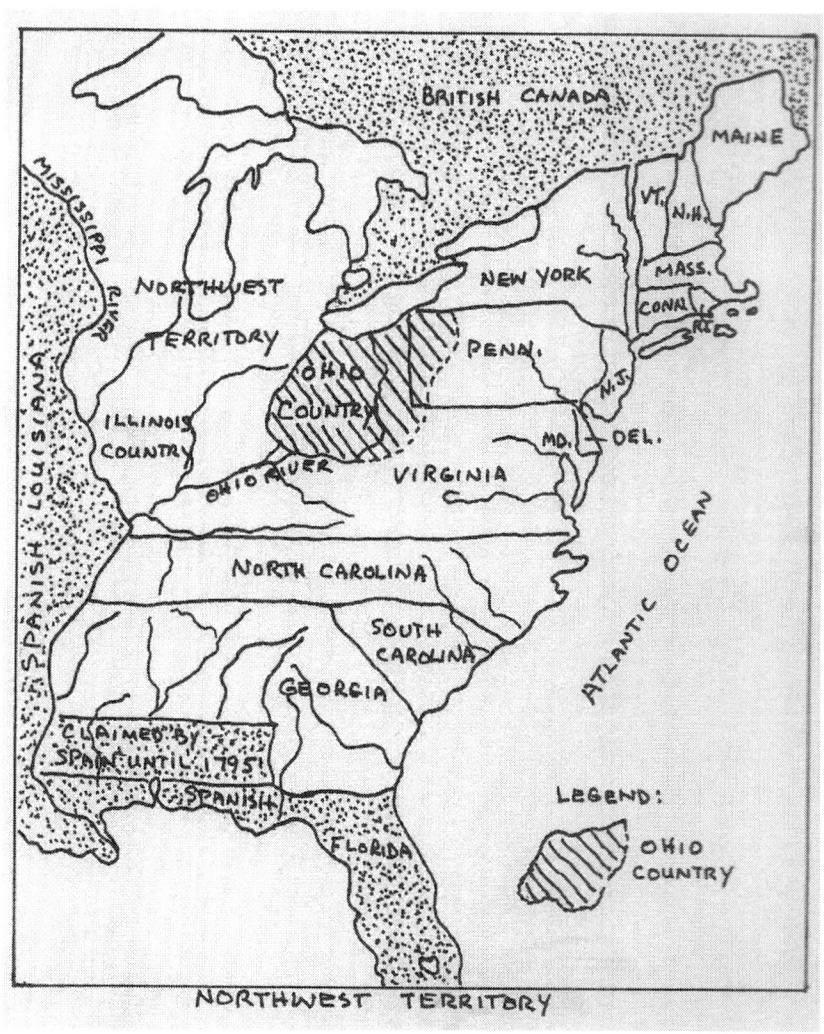

LIFE ON THE OHIO FRONTIER

A Collection of Letters
from
Mary Lott
to
Deacon John Phillips
1826-1846

JACQUELINE LOIS MILLER BACHAR

International Forum
1994

Copyright © 1994 by Jacqueline Lois Miller Bachar

All rights reserved. No part of this book may be reproduced or transmitted in any form or by any means, electronic or mechanical, including photocopying, recording, or by any information storage and retrieval system without written permission from the publisher.

Library of Congress Catalog Card Number 94-77122

ISBN 978-1-886934-01-6

Illustrations by Paul Bachar Jr.

FOR MY SONS GREG AND JOEL WHOSE TALENTS INSPIRE ME

DEDICATED TO MARY LOTT AND ALL THE
UNKNOWN WOMEN OF THE AMERICAN FRONTIER

"Once more, I lift my pen to let you know that through the mercy of Him that never sleeps nor slumbers, we are all alive and in common health."

Mary Lott

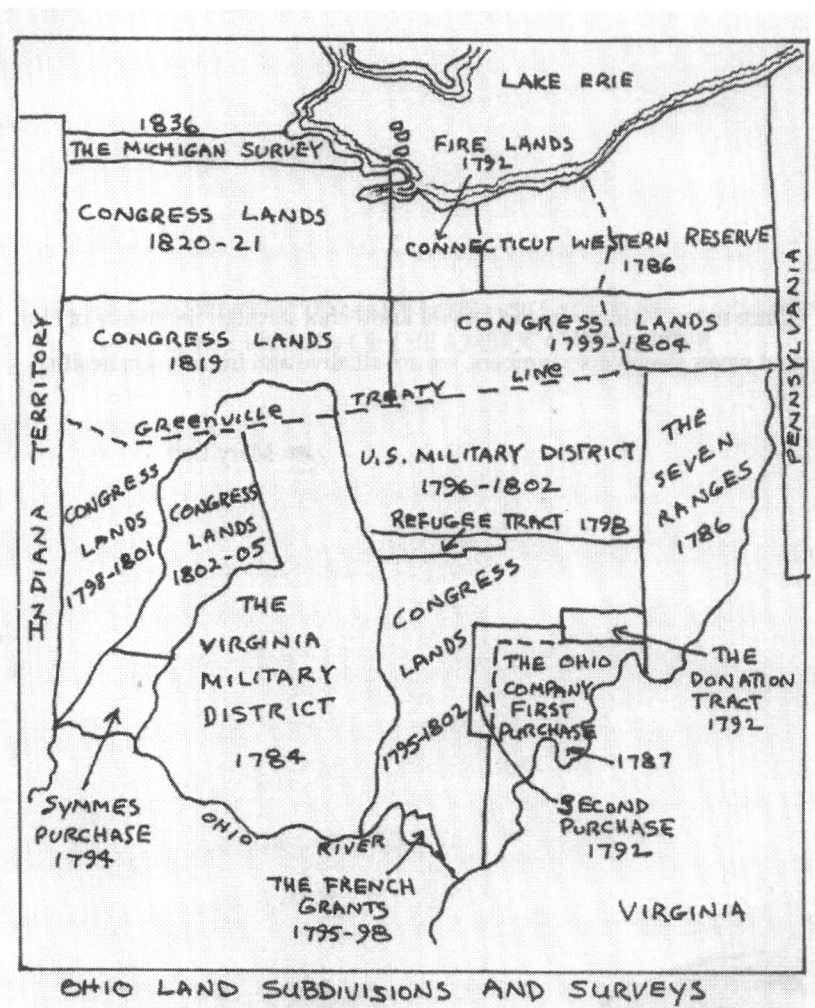

TABLE OF CONTENTS

FOREWORD	xii
ACKNOWLEDGEMENTS	xv
INTRODUCTION	xvi
CHAPTER I	
Letter - October 1826	23
Letter - February 5, 1827	28
CHAPTER II	
Letter - July 1829	33
Letter - August 7, 1829	35
Making Linen Fabric	39
Making Wool Fabric	40
Letter - December 13, 1829	42
CHAPTER III	
Letter - March 22, 1830	46
Letter – May 3, 1830	50
Letter - July 30, 1830	53
Letter - September 29, 1830	56
CHAPTER IV	
Letter - April 10, 1833	57
Letter - July 10, 1833	61
Letter – October 1833	64
Family Group Sheet - Russell Family	67
Letter - December 25, 1833	68

CHAPTER V

Letter - February 2, 1834	71
Letter - July 20, 1834	74
Letter - August, September 1834	77
Letter – November 1834	80

CHAPTER VI

Letter - August 1835	83
Letter - April 21, 1836	85
Letter - July 10, 1836	90

CHAPTER VII

Letter - February 12, 1837	93
Letter - May 15, 1837	97
Letter - June 4, 1837	101
Letter - November 26, 1837	102

CHAPTER VIII

Letter - March 5, 1838	106
Letter - January 1840	109
Letter - March 29, 1840	113
Letter -1842 / 43	115
Letter - September 10, 1843	116

CHAPTER IX

| Final Letter - March 27, 1846 | 118 |

Obituary - John Phillips ... 120
Death Dates ... 121

APPENDIX
Family of Zephaniah Lott ... 122
Lott Cemetery Records ... 123
Family of Francis Phillips ... 125
Family of Edward Williams ... 127
Williamsville Cemetery Records ... 129
Will of Henry Lott ... 132
Decline of Executorship - Mary Lott ... 134
Inventory ... 135
Will of Mary Lott ... 137
Will of Anson Williams ... 138
BIBLIOGRAPHY AND SOURCES ... 141
INDEX ... 144

FOREWORD

My original family research began with Deacon John Phillips, my grandfather, 8th generation, and his descendants. A copy of a Phillips family Bible record showed that John had a sister Mary who married a Lott. Subsequent research indicated that although John and Mary had the same father, they probably had different mothers. Therefore, I began to explore Mary's life in hopes of learning more about John through her.

The letters included in this book have been compiled from copies of the originals found in the Lackawanna Historical Society, written by Mary Lott to her brother John Phillips in Pennsylvania, over a period of twenty years. It is not known how the letters, originally in the possession of Hildah Phillips Brown, were acquired. She had researched the family of Deacon John Phillips, our common ancestor, over a period of thirty-five years from about 1935 up to her death on February 17, 1970.

To more easily identify individuals and family members mentioned within the letters, Hildah made handwritten copies, apparently to use as a notetaking tool. She added the surnames of those that she identified, made many notes, and used the various clues mentioned within to further her research. After Hildah's death, her papers were given to the Lackawanna Historical Society in Scranton, Pennsylvania.

While visiting Scranton for my research, I went through Hildah's voluminous collection and found the reprints. Although the whereabouts of the originals are unknown, the copies remain in the possession of the Lackawanna Historical Society.

Some of the letters are difficult to read and the writing is often illegible. Some parts of them have blank spaces where Hildah apparently could not read Mary's handwriting. In some cases, she has tried to decipher a word, following it with a question mark where she was uncertain of accuracy. The letters are often long and with no punctuation or paragraphs. Many are missing. In her letter of July 10, 1833, Mary refers to the fact that she has received 42 letters from John, so we can assume she wrote at least that number in response.

In preparing the letters for publication, I have made some minor changes for ease of readability and understanding. I made paragraphs where there were none, shortened sentences, and added punctuation. I was very careful, however, to do so in a way that would not affect the meaning or tone expressed by Mary. I made no attempt to correct grammatical errors except where not to do so would lead to confusion. I have corrected spelling errors except in cases where the error added a certain charm. I have also added in brackets, [*Ed. Note:*] to explain historical references and other items of clarification.

Where words are omitted or illegible, I have made additions for easy understanding. These words have been put in brackets. In instances where words are omitted or illegible, and the meaning was not clear enough for me to make additions, I have shown an ellipsis (...). The surnames added by Hildah are in brackets to separate them from surnames mentioned by Mary Lott in her writings. I have confirmed, where possible, the accuracy of these additions. In some cases, I have added surnames found during my research. These are also in brackets.

I did additional research in Delaware County, Ohio; Genesee County, New York; and Luzerne, Lackawanna and Wyoming Counties, Pennsylvania. This was done by mail and through the LDS Family History Center [now the FamilySearch Center]. I also visited the NSDAR Library and the National Archives in Washington, D.C. for further research.

Most of the people mentioned in Mary's letters are my relatives. I am a granddaughter, 8th generation, of John Phillips and am descended through Samuel Miller who married Susannah, daughter of John Phillips, and their son Stephen Miller, who married Mary Chamberlain. Others Mary refers to are great-aunts, uncles, cousins, etc.

In reading Mary's letters, I became very fond of her. I was struck by the strong religious faith she expressed. I was taken with her courage and inner strength in a time of hardship and adversity. 1 was saddened by her expressions of family longing and the ultimate fact of her facing her future alone.

I came to the decision to publish this wonderful collection of letters because I hope that individuals might learn about family connections mentioned in them. Although I have attempted to identify individuals and show family relationships, this is not meant to be an inclusive family genealogy. Rather, I hope that readers will use the facts contained within to further explore their links. I also wanted others, family or not, to share the thoughts and feelings of one for whom my affection grows and who might otherwise remain forgotten.

I know that I will not forget Aunt Mary Lott.

—Jacqueline Bachar

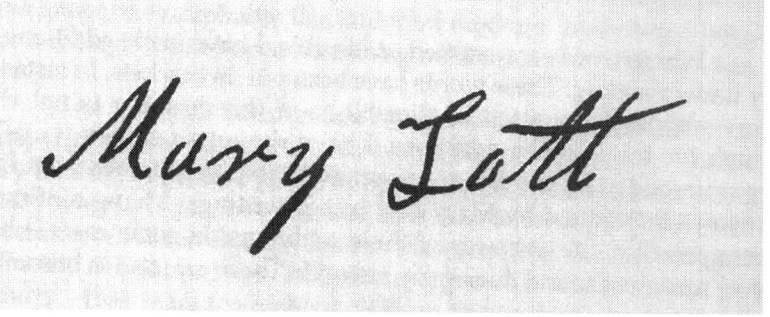

ACKNOWLEDGEMENTS

I wish to thank Maryellen Calemmo, Executive Director, and the Board of Trustees of the Lackawanna Historical Society, Scranton, Pennsylvania, for giving me permission to publish the letters of Mary Lott. Special appreciation to Assistant Director Mary Ann Moran for all her assistance. Thanks also to Marilyn Cryder, Historian, Delaware Historical Society, LeRoy, New York, for permission to publish the information from the Williams family bible. A special thank you to my husband Paul Bachar Jr., who drew the maps and illustrations, and who enthusiastically helped to search archives and cemeteries to find my family. Finally, to Hildah Phillips Brown, who started the search over sixty years ago—many thanks.

INTRODUCTION

Brief History of Delaware County

In 1803, Ohio was the first state organized from the Old Northwest Territory and it had only three counties. Delaware County, located in what was the subdivision of the U.S. Military District, was created from Franklin County in 1808. At the time of Delaware's creation, Ohio was on the frontier; Native Americans were living within county borders, and other tribes were frequent visitors right up to 1830.

The area was covered with forests. Settlers from Pennsylvania, New York, New Jersey, and New England coming into the territory established their homes in natural clearings and had to immediately set about clearing the timber. The first houses were one-room log cabins and it was many years before substantial ones were built.

Kingston Township was organized in 1813. The land was rolling, and the soil good for farming. There were no villages within the borders of Kingston then, nor are there any now. The township was sparsely populated, and the main occupation was farming, and is still.

Game and fish were plentiful. There were wild grape vines and fruit trees. Honey and maple syrup was the major source of sugar, and salt was collected from salt wells. All other necessities were grown by the population. Franklinton, now Columbus, was the closest village where settlers could take their grain to mills to be ground into flour. Luxuries such as coffee and tea were brought overland from the east and were very expensive.

In 1842, the Methodist Church established Wesleyan University, which attracted students from all over the state. The main road from Columbus to Sandusky ran through Kingston, so there were stagecoaches on a regular schedule. By 1850, with the coming of the railroad, Delaware County became a flourishing area. One of the county's famous sons became a well-known general during the Civil War. He was William Stark Rosecrans, born in Kingston in 1819 and related to the Rosecrans family mentioned in Mary Lott's letters.

—Marilyn Cryder, Historian, Delaware County Historical Society

xvii

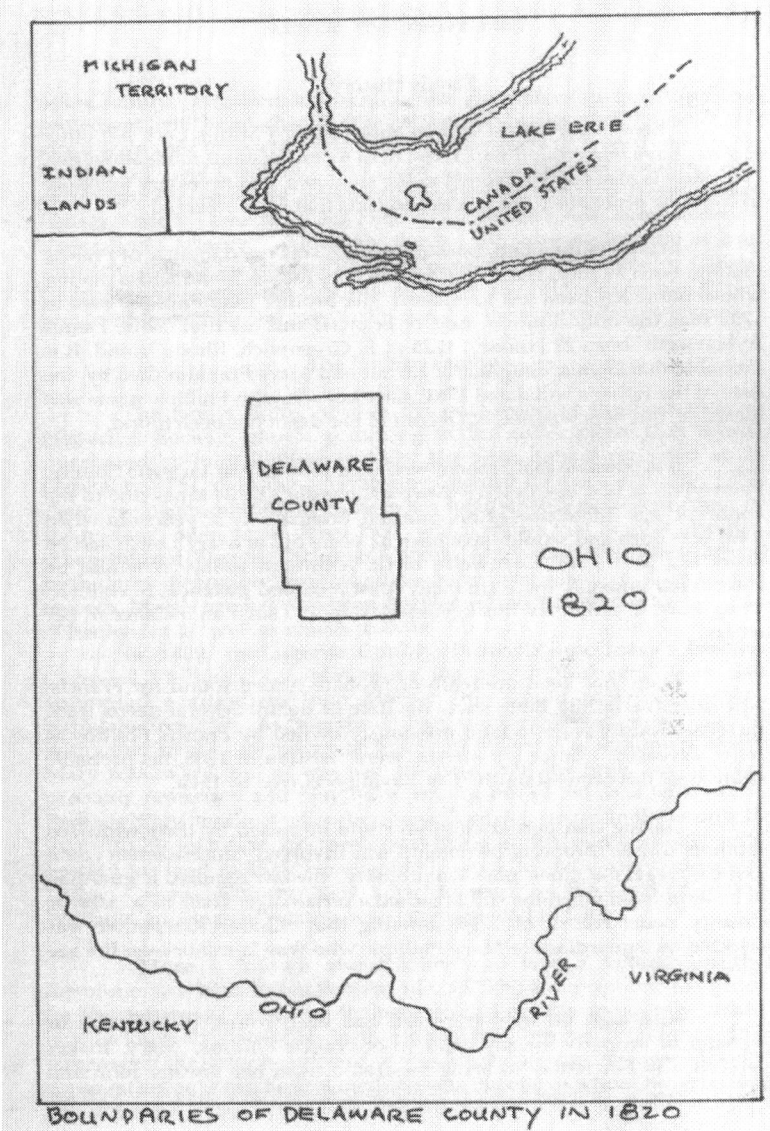

Family History

There is very little known about Mary Phillips Lott. No other records have been found which can help us understand more about her. Her parents have also remained in the shadows. It is necessary therefore to combine probability with clues and facts that have emerged.

Mary Phillips Lott, born circa 1782, was the daughter of Francis Phillips, born 29 July 1720 in W. Greenwich, Rhode Island, and a mother whose name has been lost to history. Her brother John Phillips, born in 1752. was the only known child of Francis and his first wife, Demis Aylesworth. born 22 January 1725 in E. Greenwich, Rhode Island. It is probable that Demis, daughter of Arthur and Mary Franklin, died by the date of her father's will, dated 1761, since her son John Phillips's name was included, but hers was not. No record of her death has been found.

It is possible that Francis, who probably died in Luzerne County, Pennsylvania, had been married two or possibly three times due to the apparent age differences of his children. Francis was 32 years old when John was born and would have been 62 years old at Mary's birth and 66 years old at his son Cornwell's birth. Although today it would be considered unusual, there are many past recorded instances of children being born to fathers of this age. Mary refers to such an instance in her letters.

There has been no death or probate record found for Francis, nor does the family Bible show his date of death. Several deeds from Luzerne County refer to land previously owned by Francis Phillips as "now deceased." Since the deeds were written in 1788, his probable death date has been established as having occurred by then.

During that period children could be raised by their widowed mothers unless property ownership was involved. Since women could make no legal decisions nor own property, the law required a guardian to be appointed when the child reached a certain age. There is a Luzerne County court record of 1796 showing that Gilbert Carpenter was selected as a guardian for Mary Phillips, who was "a minor over the age of fourteen."

Although no further record has been found of any sale or transfer of property for any children of Frances Phillips, Mary refers in her letters to being separated from her brother John and other family members as a child. She also refers to her hope that settlement will be reached for the heirs of the "sufferers." *[Ed. Note: This was a term used to describe people who were owners of property under the Connecticut Land Company with whom Pennsylvania was disputing such ownership. The Wyoming Valley of Pennsylvania was then Westmoreland County, State of Connecticut, and Francis Phillips was a landowner under the Connecticut Company.]* Although deeds exist showing the sale of land formerly owned by Francis Phillips, none are in the name of Gilbert Carpenter. It is possible that the property she refers to in her letters remained in dispute and eventually went to the state of Pennsylvania.

The Phillips Family

The cover page of the family Bible, now in the possession of the Lackawanna Historical Society, shows that it was purchased by John Phillips in 1803. His birth date is recorded as 24 December 1751, old calendar; the new calendar date is 4 January 1752. There are pages missing, but there is a handwritten notarized copy of the missing bible pages dated 1957, which shows that Francis also had other children: Francis, Zacheous, Thomas, Mary, Cornwell. There are no birth dates shown, but probable dates have been established by census records. Mary's age has also been established by a reference to it in one of her letters, as well as census records.

In 1800, in Luzerne County, Pennsylvania, Mary's brother Cornwell Phillips, "a minor above the age of fourteen," was also appointed a guardian, John Marcy. This would make Cornwell's birthdate circa 1786. As was the custom, children were often sent to live with other family members or bound to others. It is unknown where Mary was raised, but as was also the custom of the time, her mother probably remarried and may have moved out of the area with Mary. Perhaps Mary was sent elsewhere, and Cornwell stayed in the county to live with his guardian. Cornwell was living in the county in 1817 until he sold his land in 1828. He eventually took his wife and children to LeRoy, Genesee County, New York to work on the farm of Anson Williams, an apparent relative who later removed to Ohio.

More is known about John, who was a veteran of the Revolutionary War. In his Pension file, #S7308, a deposition was given for the purpose of obtaining the pension and he was apparently asked how he knew the date of his birth. He said, "my sister told me." It is unknown if the sister he referred to was Mary, but since she was his only apparent sister, it can be assumed she was the one to whom he referred.

Since the government required proof of facts for pension requests, and since it was the custom to record important dates in family Bibles, it can also be assumed that Mary must have provided as proof the information from the family Bible of Francis Phillips. Two Bibles were listed in the Lott inventory after the death of Mary's husband Henry, suggesting perhaps that one was the Phillips family Bible.

It is not known where Francis Phillips was living during his early manhood. John's pension record shows that he was born in (Carmel), Beekman, Dutchess County, New York. There is no record of his father Francis residing there. It is possible that he was living in Dutchess County, New York as a tenant farmer since owning land in that state was made practically impossible by the wealthy landowners. There is a record of a Francis Phillips at the battle of Kittaning, Pennsylvania in 1751. Then again, he may have been living with some of the Aylesworth family members in Dutchess County, New York until he left in 1771 to become part of the Connecticut Land Company.

According to Connecticut Land Company records, Francis was in Pennsylvania as early as 1771. Later, in 1781, he sold land to his son John. John had married Mary Chamberlain on 20 January 1771. His first three daughters were born in Pownal, Bennington County, Vermont, where he joined the militia in 1776. His fourth daughter was born in Pennsylvania in the fort that John was defending. His two sons were also born in Pennsylvania where John spent the rest of his life.

John became Justice of the Peace in Pittston, Pennsylvania in 1791 and was also on the roads committee and the committee to purchase land for the county courthouse. He was one of the original landowners in Pittston and was considered a wealthy landowner, owning thousands of acres. Over the years he made many gifts of land to his children and grandchildren. He became a deacon of the First Baptist Church in Abington. He married twice after the death of his first wife Mary and lived to the age of 94.

The Lott Family

Hendrick Lott, son of Zephaniah Lott and Else Van Pelt, was born in 1773 in Bucks County, Pennsylvania where his christening was recorded as 24 April, 1774 at the Reformed Netherlands Dutch Church, Southampton. Zephaniah Lott joined the Bucks County militia and fought in the Revolutionary War. In about 1791, he moved his family to Mehoopany, Wyoming County, where he resided until 1817 when he and his wife, with some of his children, removed to Delaware County Ohio.

There is no record of the date or place of Mary Phillips marriage to Henry Lott. There is a Henry Lott on the 1800 and 1810 Luzerne County Pennsylvania census, but it is not known if that is Henry or his father's brother Henry. It is revealed in Mary's letters that they were living in Stafford, Genesee County, New York prior to their move to Ohio. There is no other record of their time in New York State.

Nothing is known of Mary's brother Thomas. In her first letter, it is clear that Thomas travelled with Mary and Henry to Ohio, but the fact of where he lived prior to the voyage is unknown. In Mary's will, he is referred to as Thomas Simmons. If that is his middle name or if he is the child of a different marriage remains a mystery. According to the 1840 Delaware County, Ohio census, he was older than Mary, so perhaps he was a stepbrother.

Henry's grave in the Porter Cemetery in Delaware County, Ohio is marked, but the location of Mary's grave and the grave of her brother Thomas is unknown.

The Williams Family

Anson Williams was born 16 October 1781, the son of Edward Williams, born in Wales, and Jemimah Wright, who were married in 1767. Anson was the eighth of fourteen children.

He married Mary More who died in childbirth 15 April 1811, probably in New York State. There were three children from this marriage: Calley (or Sally), Jemimah, and Jerrad Sanford. Anson married circa 1811, Hannah Phillips, born 1792 in New York and who, according to one source, had resided in Pennsylvania. Although there has been no record found, it appears that Hannah was related to Mary and John Phillips. In her letters, Mary refers to Hannah as her relative, and Anson is referred to as brother Anson. Cornwell Phillips and his family also moved from Pennsylvania to live and work on Anson's farm.

In the copy of the Williams family bible, it states that Anson was a tavern owner in Cherry Valley, New York. He became an original owner of land through the Holland Land Company and is listed as a buyer in 1809. He was in LeRoy, Genesee County, New York in 1815 when he and his wife Hannah purchased land. He was owner of several properties in LeRoy, where he resided until 1836 when he removed to Delaware County, Ohio. His brother John had preceded him to Delaware County several years earlier.

He and Hannah had seven children and when they went to Ohio, they took all their married and unmarried children with them. He had purchased one thousand acres of land and planned a town called Williamsville. He was considered a wealthy man and at his death left a great deal of property to his family. He died 28 March 1847 and is buried in the Williamsville Cemetery in what is now Orange Township. Hannah went to live with her daughter Rebecca and died in 1851. She is also buried in Williamsville Cemetery.

Their son John More Williams lived on the family property until 1859 when he and his family moved to Liberty Township where they lived until his death in 1899.

Epilogue

In her will, Mary Lott left fourteen acres of land to her friend Robert Wells and ten acres to Isaac Dayton Tanner (or Tayner), the bound boy she had raised as her own. On 20 November 1848, Robert sold the land to James Stark, the executor of Mary's will. Isaac apparently kept the land until 9 December 1850 when he also sold it to James Stark. He was then living in Sandusky County, Ohio

CHAPTER I

I am none disappointed in the country. You know, I never expected to like it as well as New York State.

October 8, 1826

Direct to Kingston, Delaware Co, Sunbury Post Office, Ohio

To John Phillips, Abington, Pennsylvania

To My Dear Brother and Sister,

 I once more lift my pen to let you know we are yet in the land of the living, while many are now with the Pale Nation of the dead. My time is so short I have to write as the man that takes it, Mr. Giles, is to start in a few hours. I hardly know how to begin, but I hope you will see him. He has almost promised me to go there, but I first must tell you, we arrived here the 4th of July. We came from Buffalo [New York] to Portland [Ohio] on the steam boat; had good luck, was two days and two nights on water, but we had a very tedious journey from there in consequence of rain and new roads. We found it about 100 miles. [*Ed. note: Portland is now Sandusky, Erie County, Ohio.*]

 Henry's [Lott] and Thomas' [Phillips] eyes was very bad all the way and have been ever since. Henry's are some better, but with sorrow I must tell you that poor Thomas has untimely lost one of his and can see very little with the other. We have reason to fear he will lose that. His health is very poor. He is not able to do scarce a chore. Father and mother [Lott] have been much out of health two weeks; father with rheumatism in his knees and mother with sore eyes. They send their love to you. My health has been better since I have been here than it had been for two years. What would be done if it was not, I can't say, for the old people live in a room alone. [*Ed. note: The Phillips family bible indicates that there was a brother named Thomas. In Mary's will, however, Thomas is referred to as Thomas Simmons. No other records have been found that can explain this. Simmons may be a middle name, or he may be a half-brother or stepbrother from another marriage. Since the bible is the only record to date, we will assume that he in fact was Thomas Phillips.*]

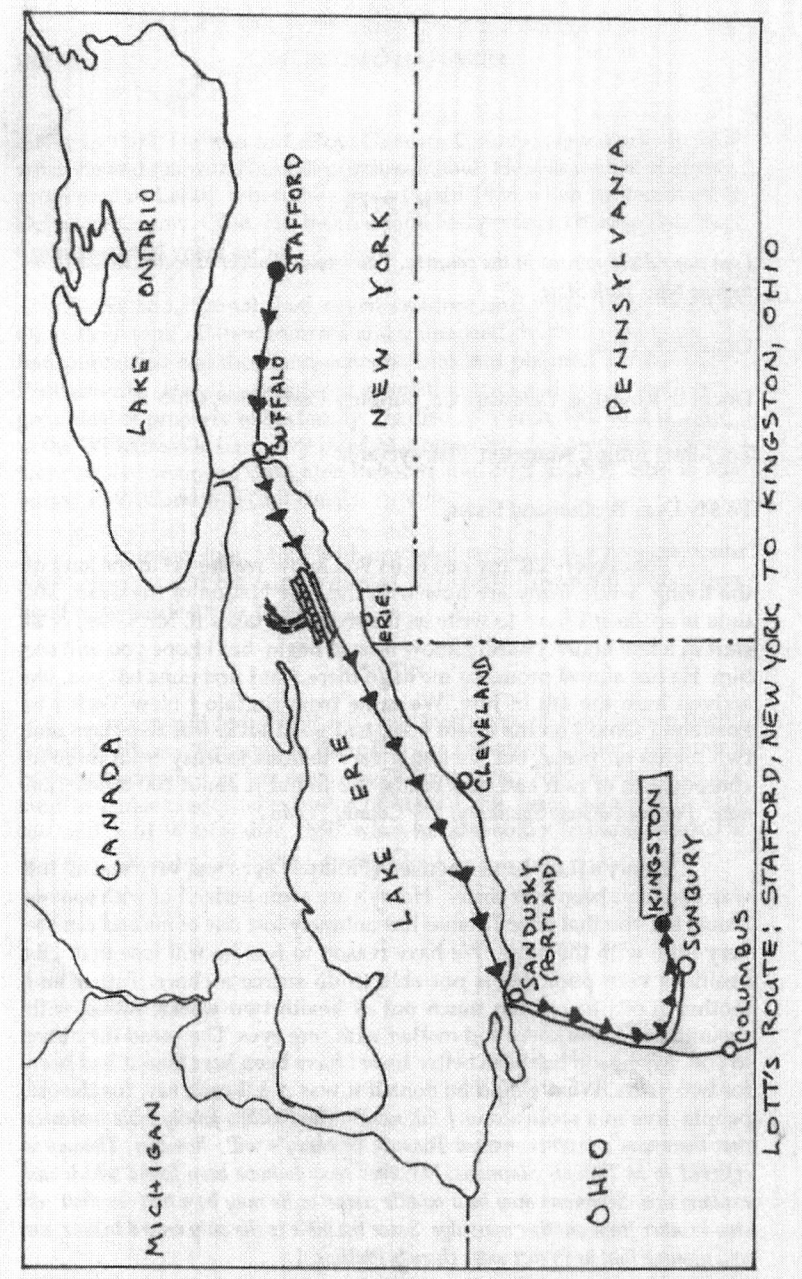

We live in an old house of his brother Leonard's [Lott] about a quarter of a mile from them. I go every day once or twice and get their victuals, and do their work up, do their washing and baking. You may ask what did they do before I come? Could I see you, I could tell you the whole story, but can now say bad enough.

Henry was much disappointed, but I was none. You know the word was, he was to go on or others would have father's farm, if we would come and take care of them, but we found it very different. It is true, we might have went on his farm, but it lies in a back - by place destitute of either roads or water and would cost almost as much to put it in repair as to clear new and we find their daughter calculates on having all at their decease.

They have lived joining them ever since they have been in this country, but the neighbors say, and I have reason to believe, the old people have done more for them than they could do for themselves. They live helpless many years. Mother has done their sewing, knitting, and the greatest part of their washing till about two years. But they now say they are... They wish they had time to take care of the old people, but I shall always have time as long as I have strength, and neither wish, nor expect any property. They all appear very kind and friendly as yet; and all Sally [Lott Carney] does is write. Father says he never met with such a daughter before, and truly I think he may ... for the rest can find but little time or otherwise, what you and I would call but little heart, for I could make as many excuses as they was I disposed...

We have bought fifty acres of entirely new land joining Leonard's [Lott]. Got two log rooms raised, the bigness of our old rooms in Stafford; [Genesee County, New York] got a well dug and mostly stoned; two or three acres chopped, but when we shall get in our house we can't say. For Henry is not very able to work in consequence of his eyes and our money most run out and fifty-nine dollars of our money we hold for we have not ... and don't know when we shall, but, however, I am not concerned but there will be some way provided the few days I have to stay. There is good provision plenty.

I am none disappointed in the country. You know, I never expected to like it as well as New York State. The inhabitants appear very friendly and meetings handy of almost all kinds, though no particular revivals of religion at present.

Poor old uncle Rosencrans [Daniel, married to Thankful Wilcox] is yet living. [*Ed. note: This name is also spelled Rosencranse, Rosencranze, Rosencranze, and Rosecrans.*] He come to see me the next day after I arrived and met me with all the affection of a parent. He lives two miles from here. He often visits me which is a great consolation to me, for he always feels bound for the Kingdom, and says he is ready and willing whenever Jesus calls. His wife and daughters are all gone; he has but three sons living. They also received me as the tenderest of brothers. You must write a word to the poor old man when you write to me, which I hope will be soon. My anxiety to hear from all of you I can't express.

I have not heard a word since last March. I have not heard from Elizabeth or Hannah [Phillips Williams] though I have wrote twice. [*Ed. note: Elizabeth may be the mother of Deborah Doud Phillips, Cornwell Phillips wife.*] I received a letter from Harriet [Trumbull] and Robert [Wells] last Friday. Harriet's husband and Robert had been sick with the fever the greater part of the summer, but was recovering. Our love to brother Cornwell and his family. Tell him I should [have] wrote, but I don't know how to direct, but he must write to me. My love to Mary; [Phillips Hewitt] tell her I seen Lavina [Hewitt Russell] when I moved. They was all well. I have wrote to them and expect an answer. My love to each child and grandchild. Accept the same yourselves. The man is waiting, so must close. [*Ed. note: Lavina is the daughter of Mary Phillips Hewitt and Isaac Hewitt. and granddaughter of John Phillips.*]

Your affectionate sister, Adieu. Mary Lott

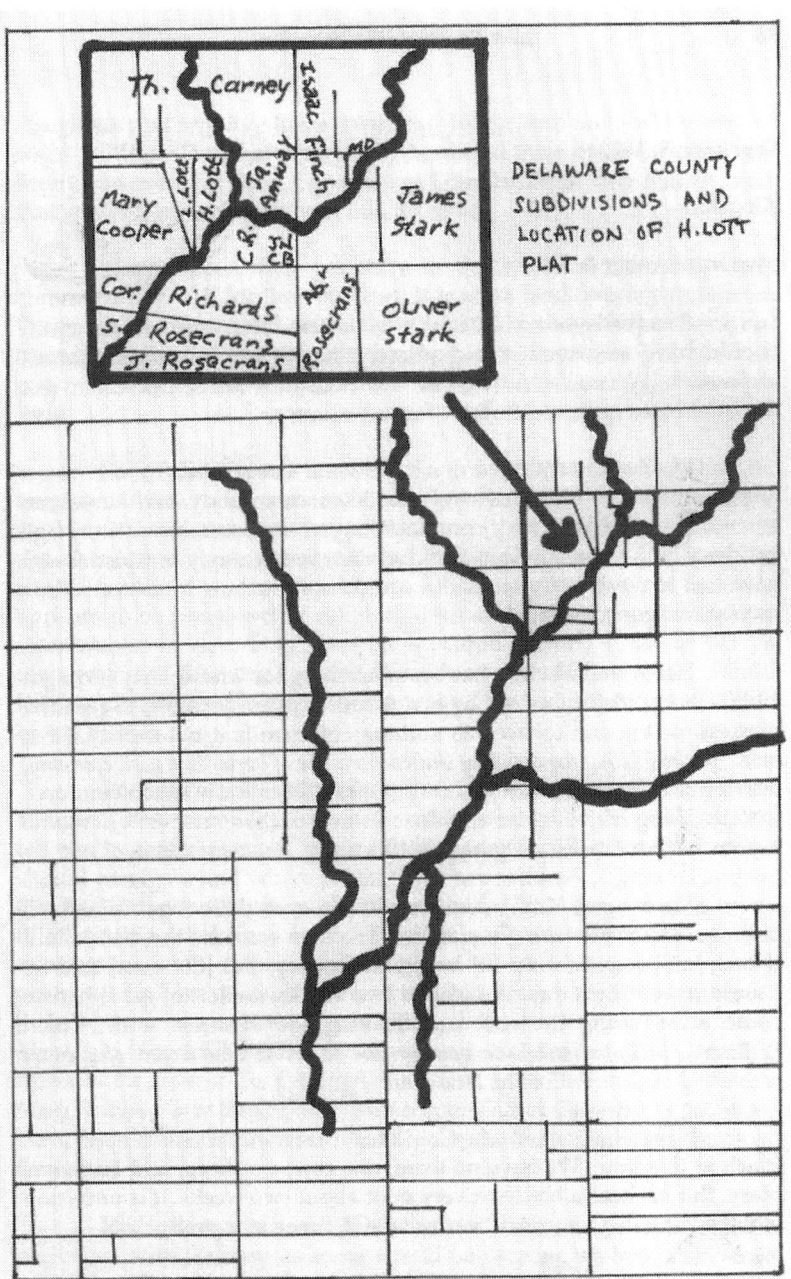

February 5, 1827

Kingston

My Dear Brother & Sister,

Received your kind and affectionate letter one month ago. I should have answered it immediately, had it not have been almost impossible. We moved in [to] our new house the 7th of December; got the front room quite comfortable for this country.

My health continued much the same it was when I wrote you a few days after we moved when I was taken very poorly, and have been so ever since. I have every complaint any woman can have of my age besides a broken constitution, yet I have not been entirely confined. But, I have had to work every moment I could for something to live on as our money was gone last fall.

Henry and Thomas has been thrashing for wheat. They have got 10 bushels paid for, but we have not sufficient for victuals; it goes the hardest for tea and tobacco as nothing commands it but money. [*Ed. note: In the 1820s, the economy shifted from one of barter to a cash economy, creating a widespread period of flux.*] I often think how much comfort I took drinking tea with you and dear sister, but them moments are gone to return no more. But, when you drink a cup, or smoke, think of me!

There was $54.00 behind on our place we did not get. I think, in consequence of not taking my advise. The man came for the deed. I told [Henry] not to give it up till he got the money, but [the man] said he should have it next day. We waited two weeks, could not get it-had to come away suing the note and leaving the business with Anson Williams. [*Ed. note: I have been unable to locate any record of a court proceeding in Genesee County, New York.*]

Henry has talked of going after it this winter as we need it so much at this time. We have no team; one cow, no sheep, and on a new place. But his health has been very poor about two weeks. It is uncertain whether he will go or not. H we can't get it, times look pretty dark.

He is much disappointed in regard to the situation of his father's family. The old people have been very [ill] all winter there by their daughters and will live there [without] living with any [of] the rest of their children. They have [it] pretty hard and their daughter can't get time to do much for them. I go often as I can [to] clean their house and that serves for cleaning at least till I go again.

They placed their property in the situation that they can't command any of it for their comfort. It is all in land, lies one mile from them; does them no good, but will not sell it. They have helped none but their daughter and she appears the most unwilling to help them, but, however, they appear content and thinking Sally [Carney] does all in sight.

Sally's family and brother Joseph's [Lott] family have had no correspondence for two years. Leonard's [Lott] wife has had another stroke of the palsy which has pretty much [deprived] her of sense and speech. He has a great trial with her. His oldest son has left him. His health is very poor, yet the care of all his family come on him. He appears to be possessed of religion, does all he can for peace and yet often strives in vain. They have all appeared friendly to me as yet in their way, but they don't seem like our sort of folks; not one I should think of placing the least confidence in, but, however, I am not destitute of real friends.

Poor old Uncle Rosencranse, the more I see of him, he seems like a father. I read your letter to him. He said I must give his love to you all, tell you he was a poor old "pilgrim" but, had got almost home where he should meet you and where parting was never known. His sons appear like the tenderest of brothers. Abraham [Roscncranse] says the tender ties of friendship felt for me in childhood when I was separated from all relatives are yet the same, and although we have been separated so many years, yet he believes with you and me that time or distance can never [break] those tender ties of friendship. [*Ed. note: It is not known where Mary spent her childhood. It is obvious she was separated from John. There is a record in the Luzerne Co. PA Orphan's Court, 1796, Vol. #1; p. 78 where a Mary Phillips, "over the age of 14" has selected Gilbert Carpenter as guardian. There is a Gilbert Carpenter on the 1820 Delaware County, Ohio census in Sunbury.*]

His wife too is good. She is as kind to me as he is, nor is she possessed with jealousy as some would be because we love as brother and sister. They have just sent me a large piece of fresh pork. They are always sending something. None of them live more than a mile and half from me. Abraham's child has been very sick since. The rest are in common health.

I have not seen Daniel [Rosencranse] since last fall. He has got to be a great ... doctor. He has many calls, so he is almost always from home. He would be pleased to see your letter, for he always inquires for you when he sees me.

We have not received any letters from Anson [Williams] or John since we have been here. I have given you a check of our situation in life. I must fill this small piece up with a bright side of the leaf. I can [bare] all my trials, griefs, sighing, and sorrowing. I feel that l have a treasure in Heaven that I soon, very soon, shall come in possession of. These reflections give me sweet consolation when all are locked in sleep with rapture. I anticipate on that happy day when the short journey of life shall end and I shall meet my dear beloved friends in the fair Heaven of eternal repose where the sound of farewells was never known.

Often of late, with most solomn reflections, l recall my past life from my childhood till the present moment; the many separations of dear friends, some by death and particular the moment, my bosom heaves forth the big sigh, while tears gives vent to my almost bursting heart, but ere, I am aware Jesus appears and fills my soul with glory and seems to say, "I am still thy friend though thorns and briars has always marked your ways. Yet, my tender mercies has been on you. I soon will take you home to rest." I then cry, Lord, it is enough! I can rejoice in adversity, while I have a few earthly friends to soothe my years. [I have a friend in] Jesus, my savior and King. I feel as though I could write all night on this blessed theme, was it proper, but my pen you see is had no knife, no eyes to mend it.

Thomas is yet blind with one eye. He sends his love to you. Often talks about you all. Henry sends his [love] to you. Fail not of writing soon. My love to each child and grandchild. I want to hear from Amzi [Wilson] and Merritt [Wilson] and Stephen Gautier. Accept my love and best wishes. Must I say farewell forever? Must I see you no more in time ... ?

P.S. We have had the hardest winter that has ever been known here, good sleighing since Christmas and about as cold as I have ever known it in [New] York State the greatest part of the time. When I read that Mary [Phillips Hewitt] had been at Lavina's and I not there, my heart I thought, must burst till tears came. I have had no letter from her yet. Do you think I ever shall? Tell her don't forget me. I fear you can't read [this].

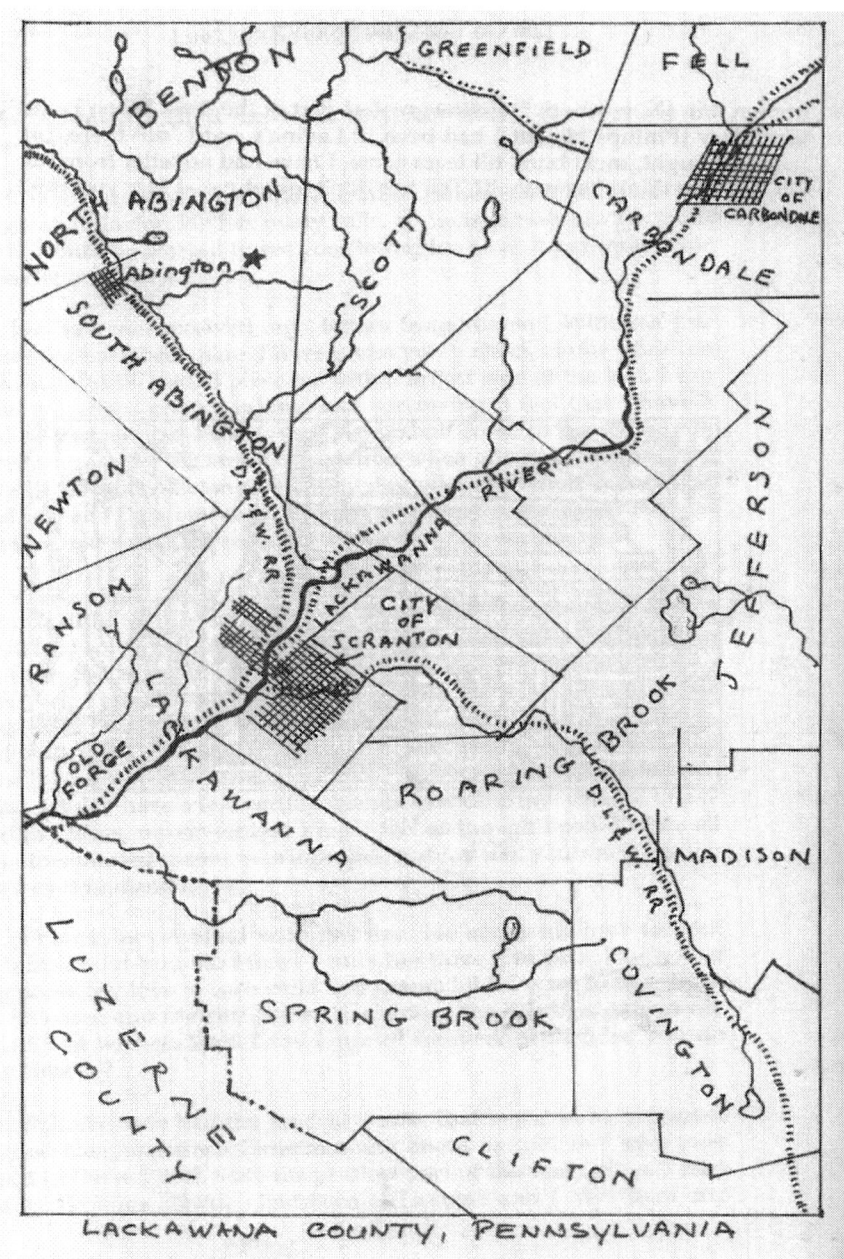

CHAPTER II

When I first read your letter, I thought I hardly knew how to be reconciled to this heavy disappointment ...

July 1829

Dear Brother & Sister,

We received your kind letter in due time. I should have answered it immediately, but I had wrote one to you and Cornwell [Phillips] a short time before, and thought I should get one from him in May. I then calculated to write. I have sent or been to the Post Office every week, but in vain. We have been looking for him and his family [for] some days. We can't but hope he started the first part of June as he calculated, but fear they had some bad luck on the road. Write immediately on the reception of this and let us know if he did start or not. If not, what is the cause? We are all in a great panic to hear from them and not from them only, but from you also. I must write in great haste as I must go or send it to the Post Office tonight, for I can't think of waiting another day. It will be wrote poor, but your goodness will over look all errors, when you think of the hand that writes and the heart that [incites].

Oh, dear brother and sister, could I once more fold you to this fond heart that has so long been the seat of pain, and have so often drinked deep of the streams of woe. But I wish not to look too much on the dark side of the leaf, but thank God, that He has given me a heart susceptible of feeling His love, and to sympathize with a friend, and also of feeling those tender ties of Heaven born friendship that unites the bleeding hearts together. For although I am separated from many dear friends, yet in solemn meditation one thought gives me sweet consolation; that although our days are separate, our hearts are one. And when this short voyage of life shall end, we shall be again reunited in that fair haven of eternal repose, where sorrow never comes and parting sounds was never heard.

I must drop this subject and tell you [that] we are all in common health. And mine, I think, has been better for two months, then it has been in since I have been in this state. Thomas' health is pretty good, but his other eye is very sore. We fear he will lose it, but hope for the best.

Mother Lott is here on a visit. Her health good as we can expect for one of her age. I think I wrote concerning Father Lott's death. [*Ed. note: Zephaniah Lott died February 26, 1829*] The rest of the family are in common health except brother Leonard's [Lott]. His is very poor. Rosencranse's people are well. Isaac [Rosencranse] buried his wife last May 7th.

We have had a very dry season here. The wheat is middling. Folks here began to harvest. Flax poor in general; some corn is good and some very poor. Henry and Abraham [Rosencranse] has planted 23 acres of which we have 1/3. Looks well. We hope Cornwell [Phillips] will be here to help harvest it. We have a [good crop] of flax. Looks pretty well. Our garden is not so good as common, owing to the drought and worms eating it, but, however, have plenty of beans and began to have potatoes. Our five acres of wheat looks well. It will do to harvest next week.

You are anxious to know about my coming there, dear brother. I hardly know what to say. I have thought [for] certain, [I] should but disappointments was always my lot. Mr. Huff has given up going. Mr. Grist and wife talked of going this fall, but the last I see, they talked quite discouraging of time. Should Cornwell come soon, I shall try very hard to come, if we all have our health and can possibly get a little spending money and a few clothes. And as I said before, I shall think I can go pretty [comfortable] and with as few clothes that [I] think you will not be ashamed of me.

It is most night and I expect to walk to the Post Office. I must close. Give my love to each child and grandchild and accept the same yourselves.

Mary Lott

P.S. Fail not of writing. I shall hardly know how to wait if Cornwell has not started. You will of course, try to see him and get this to him, but I think he certainly has started or he would have wrote to let us know. For if he can't come this summer or fall, we shall have to get someone else, as we can not live alone a great while longer, but we had much rather have him than any other. Farewell. Pray for me. I do for you. May God support you in the decline of life and spare you till we meet once more.

August 7, 1829,

Dear Brother & Sister,

I received your kind and affectionate letter this morning and admidst a thousand cares and a heart filled with sorrow and disappointment, I lift my pen to acknowledge my gratitude to you for the favor you now sent in addition to the many others I have received from your dear hand. I rejoice to hear that you are yet alive and in common health and likewise all your posterity. But the information you gave me concerning Cornwell [Phillips] fills us with sorrow and disappointment. How can I bear the thought that my dear brother should have no more stability than to sell and give us encouragement and then squander away his money and not come. The disappointment is great! And Henry feels as bad as I do.

We have both worked like dogs to get all we could to help them when they come. I told you in the letter put in the Post Office the day you wrote yours, how much corn we had planted. It looks well. We have got our wheat in the barn. It is very good. We shall [have] about 70 bushels. We have potatoes plenty for two families. Our flax is pulled and stacked. We shall have about 100 weight. We have saved 30 weight of our old on purpose for Esther to spin before the others got roted. *[See Ed. note pg. 39.]* I have got a loom wove—two pieces, and got another in. I meant to have learn't Esther to weave. *[Ed. note: Esther was probably Cornwell's daughter.]* We have lost no creature since we have been here, but a hog last winter. But, however, we have 21 big and little which we thought would be enough to fat for both families.

I should have anticipated on enjoying some happy hours with them, had I not known I was born a child of sorrow and misfortune. Disappointment always awaits me, yet I would sometimes look on the fair side of the leaf and think from the encouragement he gave us, he would come. But alas, I must now give up all hopes and to whom shall we look to smooth the moments of our declining years.

We have worked hard all our lives, but hard fortune was always our companion. The Lord in his good providence has never been pleased to give us a great stock of this world's goods for which I feel to bless his name. For if he had given me much of this world's riches, I might not have laid up my treasures in Heaven. Then I should have had my heart fixed on these low grounds where sorrows always grow. But now, dear brother, in the midst of adversity and disappointment, my soul beats high with anticipation of soon outriding the storm of affliction. Although I may never meet some of my dear friends in this world, yet, I think I have a hope that is sure and steadfast and reaches to that within the veil. That I shall meet my dearest friends that never fails on the other side the cold streams of Jordan, where I shall enjoy His presence without a dimming veil between.

When I first read your letter, 1 thought I hardly knew how to be reconciled to this heavy disappointment, but a thought soon struck my mind. That was, trust in God. He will supply all your wants. I thought that not withstanding, we were not rich. We had enough to support us through this short journey of life and what do we want more the next. And always as long as we live alone, we must work very hard and always be confined and should we live and die, so we should leave just enough for his relation to quarrel about. Henry says that they have got enough, that he has worked hard. Someone must be found that we can depend on if possible and we do believe there are such ones.

Now brother, do you think there is any of your grandchildren that would come, that we could depend on? My mind pitched on James Tripp. 1 liked him and his wife very much when I was there. I thought by his talk he had some notion of coming to this country or some other. If you think he would come, we want you should talk with him. Tell him he shall have the same chance [Cornwell] was to have. If he could sell and bring his money, he could buy land to a great advantage. Our little place would be a good home for them.

But, however, we shall leave it altogether for you to choose. 1 don't know as you will think you can spare any of them, but as you have so many, I think your heart can not withhold should any of them have a mind to come and smooth the last moments of a poor old Uncle and Aunt. Write immediately and let us know. We shall wait till we get another letter before we look out for anyone else. But Henry says, they must come this fall or beginning of winter. Don't disappoint us again, for we can't wait any longer. We must know as soon as possible that we may know how to calculate our affairs and to lay in provisions for them, 1 shall flatter myself once more of having some one of my relatives with me in a strange land, but perhaps these hopes are only raised to be blasted again, but I feel to submit to Him that does all things well.

Dear brother, I hardly know what to tell you concerning my going to see you. My heart says I must go and once more embrace my dear old brother and sister. I often regret the time you mention in one of your last letters, but in vain. We can't recall past time [if it] had [not] come [as] welcome as we expected I think if we had our healths as well as we have had, that one or both would have went this fall. I will hope yet if anyone should come from there, that would take care of the things and Thomas, we might come yet this winter. If Henry could not go with me, I should venture to go without him if I could get a chance and I think there is a probability of it. There is always a number going in the fall.

You can't think how bad poor Thomas felt when he heard that Cornwell was not coming. He had black walnuts laid up for the children, would talk about them every day as he and I was pulling flax. He would say next year, Cornwell's little boys will help me and how much comfort he should take working with them, but this conversation has come to an end.

He is still my brother. I still love him as such. He has the same place in my heart. I still feel the same ties of natural affection. He shall have my prayers that not withstanding he might have erred in judgement. My earnest prayer is that he may seek an interest in Christ and be [a] partaker of that pure and undefiled religion before God the Father, which will bring us still nearer by the blood of the lamb.

While writing, my heart sinks within me. Oh Cornwell, had I been there when you had your sixty dollars and yoke of oxen, I think a sister's entreats would have availed and you would have come, for when I think how much better it would have been for you and your family, as well as us, I hardly know how to be reconciled and sometimes reflect on myself for ever requesting you to come. For it appears that it has been the means of your selling your self out of house and home, but one thing I have for consolation, a clear conscience. I meant right and thought it would be best for both and had not the least thought that you would sell and give us such encouragement and then not come, but if I never see your face again in this world of woe, you shall have my love and best wishes and likewise your wife and children.

Tell Esther, I had flattered myself much with the idea of having her as well as the rest to wait on me, should [I] live to old [age]. My hopes are blasted, but if seen none of you more, I hope I may see you all in Heaven, when the storm of life shall end. I expected you would have written to me when you found you were not coming, but let nothing stop your correspondence. Write immediately and I will answer you.

Dear brother John, I don't, but you will think I have, forgot you, since I have been writing to Cornwell, but I have not. It seemed as though I must write a word to him and I know not how to write separately. Please send it if you don't see him soon.

I must tell you, I have found one of Uncle Isaac Allan's sons. He lives three miles from here. He is [a] preacher of the gospel and one I believe the Lord has called. We was not a little pleased when we found each other out, although I had never seen him, but I well remember his father and mother and oldest sisters. He has not heard from his Uncle Samuel a great many years. I could tell him much concerning them he had never heard. Let them see this if convenient. When you write again, write particulars about them or have them write. My love to them all.

Tell Melissa [Miller] I should like to know her husband's name. [Schwartz] I wish she would write. Our health's good as usual. It has been a common time of health here this summer, yet there is some died. I was to a funeral yesterday; a neighbor woman that had laid long with the consumption.

I could write more, but I must close. My love to each child and grandchild and accept the same yourselves. Henry sends his love and wants to see you so much. Farewell and believe me,
Your affectionate sister Mary Lott

P.S. Let me know where John Russell lives. I have wrote, but can get no answer. Anson [Williams] has never wrote a word about them. I would fair return your kiss, but you must accept this until I see you.

X and heart

Making Linen Fabric [Ed. Note]

When the flax plants were harvested, they were pulled up by the roots and left to dry in the field. They were then stripped of the seed pods, which were pressed to get linseed oil. The stalks were put in bundles under stones or other weights and roted or "rotted," by soaking in running water for about five days. This was done to make the core of the plant brittle in order to be broken into pieces so the core could be easily removed. The step of removal would be done by using a large wooden mallet in order to break the stalk and not the linen fiber. The plants would probably have been laid over an apparatus especially made for this process. It was hewn out of heavy logs of 3-4 slats side by side whose upper edges were cut thinner. Another set on top with the mallet attached also had thin edges and was hinged to the bottom piece. The top slats fit between the lower slat's openings.

The flax was laid vertically across the bottom while the top was brought down with great force to break open the stalk, at the same time not damaging the linen fiber. The same process could be done by using a heavy mallet alone. These were only the first steps, since the outer bark had to be removed by a scraping method which had to be done twice. The fibers were then combed using a hetchel, a device with metal teeth set into a wooden base. By pulling through the teeth, the flax fibers were combed and cleaned of broken fibers. It was then ready to prepare it for the spinning process to make the yarn. [*See illustration.*]

As the spinning took place, thread filled the bobbin from which it was removed and wound into knots of forty threads. One skein of linen yarn required twenty knots. The thread then had to be woven on a loom to make fabric such as canvas or sacking. It required finer spinning to make fabric for clothing. It was often mixed with wool thread to make linsey—woolsy, a commonly used fabric of the period which was used to make warm clothing and bedding.

The weaving of the fabric was then done on a loom on a base of taut, parallel threads called a warp. To make the fabric, a single continuous thread called the weft is passed back and forth across the threads. First under alternate threads and on the return over those threads and under the ones it missed on the first passage.

This is a very simple description of a very complex process, requiring a loom big enough and strong enough to withstand the strain of the various actions [*A loom could be as big as a double bed.*]. The loom also had to be made plumb and square; a crooked loom would weave crooked cloth.

Making Wool Fabric

In some respects, the making of wool fabric was less tedious. After shearing the wool from a sheep, it was cleaned and then dyed using various barks, berries, and flowers. It was then "carded" using two rectangular wooden paddles set with wire teeth. Carding is the process of pulling a small bundle of wool between the paddles gently rubbing them back and forth to mix and fluff the wool.

The small piece was then ready to be spun which is simply a method of twisting to form a thread. Seven knots or hanks of yarn made one skein. It was then ready to be used to make the fabric. The wool spinning wheel was much larger in size and much simpler to operate than the flax spinning wheel. [*See illustration.*]

WOOL SPINNING WHEEL

December 13, 1829

Dear Brother and Sister,

I have stayed home from meeting to let you know we are all in common health and sincerely hopes this finds you yet alive, and all your children and grandchildren in good health. I received your affectionate letter in due time. Was glad to hear you was yet in the land of living and as well as you are, but dear brother, the feelings of my heart on reading the situation of Cornwell's family, I shall not try to describe, but leave you to guess. I have almost given up the idea of ever seeing him or any of the rest of my relatives. I am sorry now that I ever wrote for him to come. But we thought it for the best, but may the Lord bless them whether they stay or come.

Poor John [Russell] and Lavina [Hewitt Russell]. Must adversity follow them to the grave? I often regret ever taking her away from her mother, but I meant no wrong, nor, that no hurt. Could I have looked a little ways [into the] future, I should have done different in that, as well as many other things thru life, but alas, we are short-sighted mortals and can't know the least event till it comes. Give my love to them. Tell them I shall be as glad to have them write as ever. I would, though I hardly expect it. But may they ever remember that I am the same friend I ever professed to be.

I must now tell you that when I received your last letter, l was in hopes of clasping you in my arms and pressing you and my dear Lydia to this fond heart. There was one of our neighbors going to Jersey and would go as near you as Montrose. [Pennsylvania] He gave me some encouragement for several weeks, but as there was a number going, he could not tell certain till two days before he started. And then it was impossible for us to get clothes or money on so short a notice. And it was so late in the season, I could not go without being warmly clothed and even then, I should have been afraid to have started. For it stormed when they started, and it has rained or been very cold or snowed almost every day since. There was never such a fall known here before and indeed, I never knew such a one any where. But should the good Lord spare your lives and ours, and health another season, I do believe I shall see you, if no misfortune befalls us.

We have got a good crop of flax. Got it roted and taken care of. I have got a loom. Have wove toward 100 yards this fall. Some to pay for the loom, some for spinning, a little for money. But I have got my loom almost paid for and then, if I have my health as well as I have for three months past, I intend to try for some clothes and a little money to go and see you next summer. But, I must have considerable bought, for I have had nothing out of the store since I have been in this state. Save, one black silk handkerchief; that and two of the aprons I got with the money you sent me. And you know I was not very well off when I came from [New]York State, but, however, I shall do with as little as I can.

Henry is willing I should go and would be glad to go with me, could we get anyone to leave that we could trust, but if we can't, and I can get a chance and I do think I shall, I shall go in the summer or fall at farthest. Tell Mary [Hewitt] I have seen her sister-in-law, the widow Carpenter, [Betsy Hewitt] though not since I received your letter, but she lives in the town Zoar [Delaware, Ohio]. Mary must direct to Sunbury [Ohio] Post Office and I presume she will get them, for she lives within two miles of the office. Give my best love to her and her husband and children. I would write to her, but it seems almost impossible. I have so much to do on week days, and no girl to help me, and Sundays, I must go to meeting some and even when I stay home, I can't get time to write but one, and that must be to you. I think of her often and was I in her situation, I think I should write to her and many others in that place oftener than I do.

There is Comer's [Phillips] wife [Hannah Mott] and her daughter Polly and Jabez Carey. I often think, I will write to them tomorrow, but every day brings its cares and so I must put off from time to time, but do give my love to them. I have not forgot them and likewise cousin Samuel Miller's family. [*Ed. note: This is my grandfather, 7th generation.*] You wrote that Amanda [Miller Parker] said she most had a notion of coming. I don't want to persuade, but I do almost flatter myself that if I go there she or some of the [family] will at least come home with me and see the country, and if they should like it, they would come. We have none in view any where in this country as yet. Write soon and let us know how they feel about it and let us know where my brother Cornwell is and whether you think they will ever come.

Mother [Lott] is yet living, though very feeble. The rest of our friends are all in common health. Do let me know if cousin Bates is living. Give my love to her and Joshua, Sabra and Hitty, should you see them.

Dear brother and sister, I had meant to [try] and express some of my desires. I have to once more press you to this fond bosom, but opportunity presents to send this letter to the [Post] Office. But my heart is the same and my determination is to see you, should the Lord spare our lives and health. And my prayer is, that Jesus may be your best and dearest friend, and support the tottering frames till we meet again in this life, but if not here, I fully believe we shall in Heaven when this short voyage of life shall end, and may our Heavenly Father's presence cheer us while passing through the thorny maze. Soon shall we outride the storm of affliction and our weary souls shall be at rest. I must close. My love to all. [Accept] the same yourselves and believe [I am] ever your affectionate sister,

Mary Lott

P.S. Thomas says I must send his love. He wants to see you all.

SUGAR CAMP

CHAPTER III

Don't fail of writing immediately on the receipt of this. I shall hardly know how to wait. For every letter seems almost like seeing you.

March 22, 1830

Dear Brother and Sister,

We received your kind letter a few days ago. Was rejoiced to hear you was yet alive for my heart had trembled for some time expecting to hear that you was gone to dwell with Jesus. I had been trying to pray [to] the Lord to prepare me for the doleful news of your death, for I had been worried by the feelings of my heart that some heavy trial awaited me and my mind nearly established that it was you, but although we may be warned of events by strong impressions of mind, yet they often come from a quarter least thought of and so it has proved with me.

We heard there was two letters in the [Post] Office for us. Henry went after them, returned in the evening. Came to the sugar camp where I was boiling sap. I soon knew one was from you by the writing. I broke open the other first and see James Williams name alone, marked around with black. With broken heart and streaming eyes I soon read that my beloved Sally [Russell Williams] was no more.

[Ed. note: It was the custom of the time when announcement of a death was made, it was done on paper edged in black. It appears that by the tone of her remorse, Mary knew Sally quite well and had a special feeling for her. It is possible that Sally may have been related to John Russell since her maiden name, according to the Williams Bible, was Russell. No other record has been found to confirm the relationship.]

Yes, brother, the Lord has thought best to try *me* again by laying His afflicting hand upon me and in a way I least thought of, for I had never thought but that she would live when I was gone, but He has taken her to Himself, while a tender husband and ten children are left to lament the absence of a kind companion and affectionate mother. Pray for me, dear brother and sister, that I may have this and every other affliction He shall please to lay on me with Christian fortitude, and as a good soldier of Jesus Christ. *[Ed. note: James Williams with wife and ten children appear on the 1830 census in LeRoy, Genesee*

County, New York. Shown with M; *1-under 5; 2-5 to 10; 3-10 to 15; 1-40 to 50: F; 2-under 5; 1-10 to 15; 1-15 to* 20; *1-30 to 40.*]

I must tell you that your letter gave me great consolation. It seemed as if it was sent by divine providence in that hour of deep distress as a balm for my almost bursting heart. I expect they will write John [Williams] more particulars than he did to me. I hardly know what to tell you about my coming to see you, but I can't have the thought for a moment of never seeing [you] once more and again press you to this fond heart and relate some of the sorrows I have been called to [face] since I saw you last. Henry says he don't think l can make out to go in the spring. If we live and have our health as well as we now have, he will do his best to have me go in the fall. I do have faith to believe I shall make it.

I have stopped weaving a few weeks and been making sugar in a camp by myself. I have made 75 pounds and the big one; there has been 258 made. Mine will help me to some considerable clothes and I shall commence weaving again when sugaring is over and I think I [have] prospered. I can make out money by September to have my expenses there and if I do, I shall venture to go.

[Ed. note: Sugaring is a term used to describe the process of removing the sap from the "sugar bush," a group of sugar maple trees. The sap was then boiled to make maple sugar and molasses. A separate camp was set up in the place where the trees were tapped. Later, a lean-to or small cabin was built where the process could take place out of the elements. The reference to the big camp may have been a cooperative effort among families.]

If I can light of a chance and I think there will be no doubt of that, for there is always people going from this country to that, in the fall, more than in the spring. I have some hopes that Henry will go with me yet, if we can possibly get anybody to take the care of our things. But, rest assured that if I live and have our health,] shall if he don't, and if I do, I shall make you a long visit.

Tell sister Lydia, she had better if convenient, make her visit in June, so as to get rested when I get there, for I shall depend on the cup of tea she has promised me and likewise on the hugging and kissing and sleeping and you must expect the same. You will find a little more flesh than when you hugged me last, if sickness or hard work don't take it off.

But I fear I shall go too far in anticipation while on this subject and fancy myself already in your arms. One thought quickly tells me that ere that time shall [come] round, the hand that now writes may be cold in death and with this frail body be confined to the narrow limits of the grave, or your days be numbered and perhaps both may end this life's short journey.

Well, dear brother, should this be the case, I still retain a strong hope that we should meet on the fair banks of everlasting deliverance where we shall feel no more pain, sorrow, grief; nor disappointments shall reach us, but there we shall hail all those dear friends that have gone before together with the good ... prophets and apostles that have bore the Cross while here below, and have entered into that rest prepared for all Lord's dear children. There we shall behold our dear Redeemer that died on the cross that we might live. Oh, the boundless love of God! My soul admires His long lengthened goodness particular to me, an unworthly worm of the dust, that I am shamed when so many of my friends and relations that have gone even in the bloom of youth. Fain would I write more on the pleasing theme of God's love toward fallen man, but paper and time would fail me.

Mother Lott is yet living, though very feeble and almost helpless. She was very sick last winter. We were called two or three times; they thought she was dying. But we think she can't stay long with us. The rest of the family are in common health. Abraham Rosencranse and family are well. Daniel [Rosencranse] has not returned from Canada and Michigan. We have heard he was well and was calculating to come home in the spring.

It's quite a healthy time. I know of none sick near us. We had some pretty light weather last winter. Good sleighing for near one month. The spring has been favorable so far and there's not much appearance of even any more sugaring at present. Thomas' health has been better this winter than any winter since we been here, except he is troubled with rheumatism. My love to Elder Miller. *[Ed. note: Elder John Miller was not related to the Miller family in these letters. He was born in Voluntown, CT February 3, 1775, and came to Abington, PA in 1802. Elder Miller bought 326 acres from Deacon John Phillips for $40.00; $20.00 to be paid in money when "he could do so as well as* *not," $10.00 in maple sugar, and $10.00 in tin ware. He was the first pastor of the Abington Baptist Church and remained so for over fifty years. He officiated at both the second and third marriage of Deacon Phillips.]*

Tell him, I have not forgot him and by the grace of God, I expect to meet him in Heaven when life shall end and conflicts cease. Give my love to James Tripp, his wife and children. Tell him, I hope he will sell his farm and conclude to come home with me next fall or winter, but I hope he will not make out as poor Cornwell [Phillips] has. I am not afraid in the least that he will, but poor brother, my heart aches for him and his wife and children. If you should [write to him], tell him I am the same affectionate sister, but I fear for him should he go to Anson's, [Williams] but I hope for the best.

My love to John, [Russell] Lavina [Hewitt Russell] and their children and to each child, grandchild. I can't name them all, but you know my heart. Let me know in your next letter who lives with you, and if they are kind to you and my dear sister Lydia. Write soon. Let me know your health and I shall keep writing to let you know how I make out in getting things for my journey and what time I shall start. Henry is well, sends his love to all. I hardly know how to say by my pen, although have wrote so long [a] letter, but paper fails.

I haste to send my love to you and Lydia and subscribe myself your affectionate sister,

Mary Lott

May 3, 1830

My Ever Dear Brother & Sister,

I received your welcome letter dated April 13th, the 1st of May, and dear brother, every letter I receive from you I press to my bosom and return thanks to our Heavenly Father for His loving kindness in sparing your life so long. Every one I fear will be the last I shall receive from your hand, but I do pray, and I think in faith that your lives may be spared and fortune smile on me who was born one of sorrow's children. That we may once more meet in this world, and once more have a kind of mournful pleasure in relating some few joys and our many griefs while we have been passing thru this veil of tears.

Me thinks I can see you and my dear Lydia now, sitting in that room alone, and did I not believe that Jesus was your friend, and religion your consolation, I should feel very different when I think of you and know how near you are to the silent tomb, but one sweet thought arises, that is death to the saved means no more than a black curtain drawn to let our souls go in, and the faster these frail bodies are drawing to the grave, the nearer our souls are drawing to the portals of Heaven and ever lasting happiness.

And when we have entered there, we shall meet our departed friends and see our dear Redeemer without a dividing veil between, and bid adieu to life's dull cares and leave all our griefs, sorrows, pain and woe behind. But not withstanding the strong and pleasing idea I entertain of meeting you in Heaven, the desire of meeting you once more in time still keeps kindling in my breast and some time I think I can not be denied.

You told me you was [coughing] much stuff up [from] your lungs. If I was there, I think I could make a syrup that would [help you.] Tell her I wish she would make you one. If Lydia is not able, take hoarhound, hysop, wild cherry bark, dog wood flowers. Boil them very strong, strain it out, add to it half spirits. Take three or four times a day as much as you think you can bare, with honey if you have it, if not sugar will do. It will take a great deal more than you think, for I am sure you will find benefit by taking it. Tell them I hope they will try and nurse you up that you may live till I come, for I still feel determined if the Lord spares our lives and healthy [to come] in September. [*Ed. Note: Hoarhound is of the mint family, from which a bitter juice is extracted to make a cough medicine; hyssop is also of the mint family used as a tonic, stimulant, etc.*

You wished to know how I am like to get along as to my clothes. I have got a few since I wrote last, but must have more, but hope I shall get them. As to money, I have none. Yet I have two very nice calves, one of each kind, the big breed. I shall sell them. They will fetch money though, to be sure. They are lean, but it will be some. And I have a good hog, about a year old, that will fetch a little more, but I expect all I can get will be very scanty enough. I know of no chance yet, but I believe I shall come, some how.

I heard this morning that Peter Stephens and his wife was certain going in September. They live in Johnstown about twelve miles from here. I shall try for a chance with them and I think there is no doubt I shall succeed if I can possibly get money to pay them before I go. It is true I see no way at present to get enough, but I will trust in Him that has always provided for me, knowing he is just the same. ff I go with them, I expect they will take [me] as far as Wilkesbury or Kingston [Pennsylvania] and if there is no other way, I can soon walk to you, if it was as far again.

My health is yet quite good for which I do feel thankful. Henry's health is also good. He sends a great deal of love to you and Lydia and wishes it was so he could go with me, but I fear it won't be possible. If we had anyone we could depend [on] to come here to take care of the things, he would go. Thomas is well. He sends love to you, wants to see you, often talks about [you].

I read your letter to Mother Lott. She said I must send her love to you. Poor, old woman, she is entirely past labor and almost helpless and fears she will be called to another severe trial. Her daughter Sally [Lott Camey] that she lives with, has been out of health all winter and she can work but little and looks as [if] she would stay but a short time if she don't get help. If she should die, I expect mother would want to come here, but I have told Henry, I should not agree to be disappointed of seeing you on that account, nor does he wish me lo. They have given all their property [lo] their son-in-law and they must take care of her at least till I come back. If I undertook to take care of her, I should never have a thought of going, but make up my mind to have stayed with her as long as we both lived.

It is a general time of [good] health. Our neighbors are generally well. Don't fail of writing immediately on the receipt of this. I shall hardly know how to wait. For every letter seems almost like seeing you. Let me know if you are taking anything to try to keep you up. Do try to get everything you can think of to keep that dear frail body alive till I come; that I may once more embrace it before I die.

My love to John and Lavina [Russell] and their dear little ones. How I long to see them. And Lois [Miller] and Polly [Felts]. [Ask] if they have forgot their Uncle Henry and Aunt Mary. I received a letter from Anson [Williams] not long since he wrote. He was better now. All in common health, but expected Hannah would be sick in April or May. *[Ed. note: Hannah's daughter Rebecca was born June 20, 1830]* Monday last, I got one from James [Williams) and one from Nancy [Williams]. Poor girl, she wrote most affectionately on her dear mother's death, that I ever see anyone [do] in my life. Her health is yet poor. She thinks she shall soon meet her dear mother. May Jesus support her through life and be with her in death. Tell John and S ... if they don't write to me, they must to them. You see, my paper is gone. I can but say, my love to all and believe me yours forever. Farewell.

Mary Lott

July 30, 1830

My Dearest and Best Brother and Sister,

I received your long expected letter two weeks ago with great joy. I read that you was yet alive and some better than when you wrote before. I should have answered it next day, but have been to see those I expected to go with, but they have all given up going. But, I don't despair yet, for I feel as though I could not be denied once more embracing my dearest brother and sister and pressing you to this fond heart.

Now I know but one way, and I am almost ashamed to say. For in going that way I must be under the necessity of requesting more of what your liberal heart and hand has so often bestowed on me. But dear brother, you must consult your own interest and feelings and be sure I shall not think hard if you can't find it convenient to assist me and [it] finely prove so that I could not come. But if you could send me perhaps seven or eight dollars, and I don't know but less might answer, I could get to Portland *[Ed. note: Now Sandusky, Erie County, Ohio]* and then get on the steamboat to Buffalo [New York] and then on the canal or stage which ever was the cheapest, and some think it would be full the best way for me. And I should go a great deal quicker than any other way.

I have got a letter wrote to send to brother Anson [Williams] and as he writes that he wanted to see me much, I gave him a sly dun, telling him what you had sent me [and] was his heart as large as his purse. I might expect some from him, but as it is, I dare not look for much, if any, at least. I dare not put any dependence on it at present, but, however, I shall be preparing to go till I get another letter from you, which I shall expect as soon as possible after you receive this. For I intend to start the first days in September if the good Lord spares our lives and health which I hope and pray he will.

Our health is good at present. Thomas has had a bad turn of the rheumatism, but has got over it. I have not sold my calf nor hog yet, but they look well and several want them, but I shall keep them as long as 1 can. No danger but they will bring the money anytime, but I must have some things that 1 can't do without. I have got me a new bonnet and frock and shoes. I shall get as little as I can go with, anyways decent.

I have got a housekeeper engaged; Henry's niece, and a very fine girl she is. She can weave and do any kind of work. I have no weaving engaged, but one or two small pieces, but what seems to be the [emphasis] about my work is to get me a mantle *[Ed. note: a hooded cape.]* which I must have. But I have got contours, warp to fill my wool on, and I am calculating to sell the doth and buy one out of the store as I can't wait to have it invested. *[Ed. note; contours is part of the weaving equipment.]*

Although I enjoy pretty good health, yet some how or other, I can't get along with my work as I did in the winter and spring, but I don't see as I lose flesh. I was weighed not long since and weighed 119 [pounds] which is the most I have in 18 years, but I fear I shall lose some before I see you, but perhaps not.

I expect to lose the help of my friend Robert Wells. I don't know if I have mentioned him to you lately. He has been here more than a year, has helped [me] a great deal as his health has been better than it has been for many years before. But, he has just received a letter from his sister Harriet that brought the news of the death of his father. He died with Harriet on the 23 of June. She has no brother or sister near her and Robert thinks he must go to her. He will start in a week or two.

I have had a letter from James Williams and another from his daughter Nancy. They write that Anson's folks were all in common health and that Cornwell's family were well. We have had a good harvest and got it cut and put in the barn; a royal crop of flax; got it pulled and stacked. Our corn looks middling. [It] is not so good as other years owing to the wet weather last spring.

Mother Lott is yet living and she and all the rest of the family are in common health. I guess Squire Daniel [Rosencranse] has not returned from the Michigans. His family and the rest of the Rosencranses are in common health. The dysentery is now prevailing and pretty mortal, particularly among the children. Almost every day, we hear of more or less dying, but as yet there has been none in our neighborhood. But, how soon it will come, God only knows.

Give our love and best wishes to John [Russell] and Lavina [Hewitt Russell] and their dear children. I am glad to hear it is as well with them as it is, and I fondly hope in less than three months, I shall see them and the rest of my relatives in that country if the Lord please. But, however, brother, I don't wish you to help me to one cent of what you will want, or against the will of one child or grandchild, for I should want to meet them all with open arms and hearts. My love to everyone of them I can't name them all.

I don't expect I shall write again till a few days before I start, unless something special takes place that I can't come. But, if I do come, I shall write the day I shall start and the letter will get there before I shall.

Farewell dear brother and sister. May God preserve your lives that [we] may once more meet in this vale of tears. If not, I expect to soon meet you on the fair banks of final deliverance, to walk the streets of the new Jerusalem, to hail our friends that have gone before, to gather with all the ransomed of the Lord, where parting sounds were never heard. Believe now and forever, that same little affectionate sister,

Mary Lott

P.S. Henry and Thomas send their love to you. Also Robert Wells sends his in particular to John and Lavina [Russell]. He has not forgot them. Let me know how Lavina is and what she has got. *[Ed. note: Lavina had a daughter named Lavina Sarah Russell, b. 1830]* May the Lord ever bless them. Direct your letter to Sunbury Post Office. Let me know if you have taken your syrup and if has helped your cough.

Kingston, September 29, 1830

Dear Brother and Sister,

I expect long before this, you have been looking for me, but I will tell you all the reasons when I see you, which I expect will not be many days after you read this. If nothing in providence takes place, I expect to start tomorrow morning. I shall go to [New] York State and whether I shall stay at Anson's or not is uncertain.

I am going with Daniel and Isaac Finch in a wagon. They are going after their mother and aunt Eunice that lives twelve miles this side of Ithaca [New York] from where I must take the stage as far as Stephen Lott's seven miles from Tunkhannock. [Pennsylvania] I think he will take me to Joshua Bates and he, I think, will go with me to your house. If not, I shall leave my trunks and go a foot, if the Lord spares my life and health as well as it is now.

Henry and Thomas is well and the rest of the family connections, although it has been [a] very sickly time in this town for some time with fever and dysentery and a number of children have died. It seems to abate of late.

I received your letter thirty days after date which was the longest that ever one has been acoming which was one reason I could start no sooner. Another was, the day I put my last letter in the Post Office, Henry fell from a wagon.

I desire an interest in your prayers that Jesus may be with me and conduct me safe to the arms of my beloved brother and sister. And may He preserve your lives and the lives of your posterity. I will praise His name forever. Farewell. When you read this, I hope I shall be no great distance from you. I remain your affectionate sister,

Mary Lott

[Ed. note: Because there are letters missing, there is a period of three years between this letter and the next. We can only assume that since Mary wrote this letter just a day before her planned departure, she did indeed complete her journey.]

CHAPTER IV

...when you read this, can your hearts tell the feelings of mine, for this moment that doleful thought has again took possession and the sound is never, no never, alas never, going to behold the faces of those I love...

April 10, 1833

Dearest and Best Beloved Brother and Sister,

With streaming eyes and I am sure trembling hand, I sit down to try to answer your kind letter that I received two hours ago. Henry went to Sunbury yesterday to mill and took it out of the Post Office. He stayed with Harriet [Trumbull) last night, and came home just as I was getting breakfast, but the breakfast was delayed, for l had to read the letter and cry sometime, before I could think of anything else. Though Harriet had read it, for she could not a letter from you in the house all night and not have read it, and they done right.

It was a letter truly of grief and joy, mingled together. How true it is, dear brother and sister, that each sweet must always have its bitter. Had I not read of my dear Jabez Carey's death, and the state of Sally [Tripp) Clark's and Amzi's [Wilson] wife's [Phelena Wetherby] health, my poor heart would almost run over with joy to receive another kind letter from that dear hand that has so often pressed me to that fond breast, capable of feeling, and enjoying all the tender emotions that human heart can feel.

I now burst forth tears, afraid for that doleful thought has again took possession of my poor heart never, never, no, never. Oh, how can I write it, never shall I behold your dear face again this side the grave. Must I never press you more to this throbbing heart? Well, dear brother and sister, though distance must divide our bodies, the remainder of our days, yet there is one sweet consolating thought. That is our pilgrimage will soon come to an end, and through the merits of our dear Saviour, I yet have a strong hope of meeting you on the sunny banks of final deliverance, where we shall hear no parting sound, no sorrow, no grief, no sickness nor pain. But Jesus' soft hand shall wipe the tears from all faces, and we shall forever behold his dear face without a dividing veil between.

We are at present all in common health except colds that we got while making sugar. We had a pretty tough time of it the last time. We never ate, nor slept in the house seven days and eight nights. We made 357 pounds of sugar and about five gallons of molasses.

Two weeks ago today, I wrote you a few lines and sent by Gardener Wilcox. He promised to take them to you, but I expect you will get this before you do that, for he was helping [to] drive horses and was going to the Jerseys and also New York City and will return that way and stay some time about the plains to visit his mother, brothers and sisters. I told him not send the letter to you, but to leave it with his sister, Jane till he come back.

I also wrote a letter to her and told her she must go with him to see you. I expect she certain will, for she promised me she would before she come back to Ohio. We expect her to come with Gardener and her brother Gilbert that is going to move here sometime in the course of the summer. You must take all the comfort you can they are there and I am sure you will think of me. Should I live to see them here, it will be the nearest like seeing you of anything I ever expect, except your letters.

It is a general time of health in the bounds of our acquaintance at present. I know of but two sick. One is Josiah Rosencranse's wife ... of Squire Daniels. She has been sick almost two years and is no better. The other is John Smith's oldest daughter Rachel. They live in Sunbury. They are very particular friends of mine. She has got the consumption. We don't expect she will stay long. I am going to stay with her tonight.

If I get your letter and one to Silas [Carey] done [in] time enough, [then I can get] to put them in the Post Office in the morning. We have had such a winter as it has been with you, but it has been pretty cold for several days. Last night it froze very hard and is quite cold today. We fear it will keep on till it kills all our peaches. The trees are just getting in blooming.

Henry has just gone to see his poor old mother. She is very feeble and helpless and nothing but a child. Brother Leonard [Lott] is quite feeble this spring, but has been so many years. The rest of our friends are in common health.

Samantha [Lott] is very thankful to you for letting her know about her uncle David. [Silsbee] sends her love and best respects to you and him should you see him and wishes he would write to her. Harriet [Trumbull] and her family is well. She sends her love to you and says she shall always love you, although she never has had the happiness of seeing you.

Robert [Wells] was here last night. He said I must give his love and best wishes to you and all your friends. I was at the [house of] Samantha's [Lott] daughter day before yesterday and read your letter to her and her husband. They both send their best respects to you and finely, all my friends that I read your Jetter to says, give my love to him and his wife. Poor Thomas sits by me now. He says give my love to brother and all the rest. Tell them I want to see them, but never shall.

Winter grain looks well. Fodder is rather scarce. We shall make out and get along. I [think] pretty well. We have one nice calf and expect two more. We also have five Jambs and fifteen odd sheep and have let Robert have an ewe and lamb, all of the one ewe that father Rosencranse gave me six years ago.

My love and best wishes to Silas and Sally Clark, to Nancy and Aurora, oh, could I but see them once more, but it must not be. But, may we meet in Heaven is my sincere prayer. Oh, my dear Sally, as your health is poor, look to Jesus for strength. May he give you living faith and grace to support [you] in the hour and article of death, land you safe of the other side of Jordan in the harbor of everlasting rest.

Our love to John Russell and Lavina and children. I wonder they don't write. I have not heard from Anson [Williams] or Cornwell [Phillips] since I wrote to you. My love to Polly Millard, to Polly Felts and her husband. I long to hear how they do. I can't name them all, but if you see my dear Mary, [Phillips Hewitt] give my love to her. Tell her I think she or Isaac [Hewitt] might write. Remember me to all your children, grand and great-grand children you see and accept our love and best wishes and believe us now and forever, your unworthy, yet affectionate brother and sister.

Henry and Mary Lott

P.S. I hope you will get your new pension. We expect Mr. Williams will get his and it will come good for he needs it in his old age. Do write and let me know all about it. [*Ed. Note: This is John Williams, born in 1734. No record has been found to indicate that he was related to the Anson Williams family.*]

July 10, 1833

My Dearest and Best Beloved Brother and Sister,

I have sit down to try to answer your most kind and affectionate letter which I received a week ago. My heart leaped for joy [at] the first glimpse I had of the writing, well knowing whose dear hand it was that wrote it. For I had been looking for some time and begun to fear I should never receive another from your dear hand. Glad as I was to know you was yet alive, when I see the black seal, my heart trembled while the seal was breaking. I said it is my dear sister Lydia or Sally Clark, but, poor David, him, one the least thought of and one I have so often pressed to my bosom and so oft carried in my arms as I lived there when he was born.

I have received no letter from Silas [Carey I yet, but will think I shall. Do let me know where he lives and where his mother lives and if you ever see or hear from them. Not withstanding your letters sometimes bring bad tidings, there is but One that knows the consolation they give my poor heart.

Two weeks ago today, Henry and I was prevented from going to meeting by rain. I took down my letter box, picked yours all out, looked at the date, read some, beginning at the oldest date and so laid them regular in one end. I had 41 before I got the last which makes 42. I keep them choice and consider them very precious, for in reading them, they are always new and sometimes in perusing them, I almost for a moment fancy myself in your arms, but alas, the next thought tells the distance that divides our bodys and my heart begins to [burst] while my bosom must ever heave for the big sigh, when the doleful thought ushers in that I must never, no never, behold your face nor hear your voice. But, I submit myself to the will of our Heavenly Father, that is too good to do wrong.

Gardener Wilcox and Jane got back last Tuesday. She said she saw you not long before she started. You was in common health. It done me good to see one that had so lately seen you, but alas, it was not seeing you myself. But, I must drop this subject at present as you well know the feelings of this poor heart and give you some information of things in these parts.

We are at present all in common health. I been very unwell with a disorder that has prevailed in this neighborhood. Twas something like a very bad cold, but I am now better. The widow Bartley died with it about five weeks ago. I think she might have lived had she have had care and things for her comfort in the first of her sickness, but help was afforded too late. I was sick at the same time and did not get there quite a week before she died. But, she died in the triumphs of a living faith and fondly committed her four little children in the hands of the Lord, saying she knew He would take better care of them then she could.

The town of Bennington [Ohio] has promised good places for them all. How many witnesses we have that there is a divine reality in pure religion, for that alone will make us willing to resign the nearest and dearest delights we possess below the sun for the sake of dwelling with Jesus, our dear Redeemer.

The season was much the same till the date of your letter. It was there since then. There has been considerable rain, but corn looks pretty well. Henry says he never had any look quite well since we have been here. We have five acres on our own land and five acres on shares. Wheat is very good this year. People are harvesting. We have five acres; looks well, It is not quite fit [to] cut. Henry is now helping Mr. Trumbull, Harriett's husband, and he is to help him. They are all in weak health and read your letter and send their love and best wishes to you and want to see you. Samantha [Lott] and family is also well. Sends her love and many thanks to you for letter to her about her Uncle David. She still wishes to be remembered [to] him and wishes him to write to her.

You wrote concerning James Ross. We return our many thanks to you for your good advice, knowing you are older and have seen more of the world than we have. But, be assured, dear brother, that we have seen enough of old people suffering in consequence of putting their property out of their hands, that was he the best man in the world, he, nor no other, would get what little we have till we have done with it, for had we naught but a cow and three legged stool, we would call it our own while we live. But we shall be truly glad to see them, for they treated me well when they brought me from your house to Stephen's and Isaac Lott's and I think they will do as well in this country as any other, work or no work.

Oh, dear, how I wish Polly and Thomas could come with them. Don't you think Stephen Miller [*Ed. note: My grandfather, 6th generation*] would spare one of his girls as I think it would be a good chance for them to come. You did not write a line about my dear Mary [Phillips Hewitt] nor has she or Isaac [Hewitt] wrote a word. Do give my love to them. Tell them I have not forgot them if they have me. Tell me the name of Tryphena's husband and where they live for I have never heard. *[Ed. note: If this refers to Tryphena Hewitt, her husband's name is Lee.]*

Poor Sally Clark; I often converse and embrace her in my imagination, but alas, it is but a vision as it was not to be [a] meeting in this world I fear, but my soul rejoices to hear she is calmly resigned to the will of God. May she hold out and hold on till she arrives to the end of the race, and she will receive a crown of life. My love to her and all her family. I can't name them all, but I love them all and remember them all.

But, I shall soon close. It is now almost five o'clock, and I must go to Sunbury tonight and stay to John [Williams] and carry some butter; put the letter in the Post Office in the morning; get me a little tea. Rachel Grist was buried five weeks ago. I have not seen one of them since. She also died very happy in the Lord.

It is the same [with] John Williams that married Sarah Brown. He is well and got his pension. I should like to know if you got yours. Uncle Crandell Wilcox came in with Gardener and Jane [Wilcox]. He has bought and is going to move in the spring. I have not heard one word from Anson [Williams] or Cornwell [Phillips) since I wrote, but am looking for a letter every day.

Mother Lott is in usual health, but entirely helpless. The rest of the connections - well. It is seasonal time of health around, yet we hear of some dying. I must close by entreating you not to fail of writing soon, for I shall wait with the greatest anxiety to hear from Sally [Clark] and others. You know who [should] accept our love. Farewell, dear brother and sister. I am yours forever.

Henry and Mary Lott

October 1833

Kingston

My Dearest and Best Beloved Brother and Sister,

Through the goodness and tender mercy of our Heavenly Father, I am permitted to answer your kind letter which I received two weeks ago. But dear brother, the feelings of my heart when breaking the seal, I shall not attempt to describe. I went in the shop alone. I soon found that my dear Sally [Clark] was gone. Tears gave vent to my poor throbbing heart before I could read the next.

My heart, I think can sympathize with the ... friend. Poor Silas [Clark] and Amanda [Miller Parker]. Me thinks I can see them in their lonely houses, the places that once divided their sorrows and doubled their joys are now empty. All those feelings I can realize from experience. It is true, I have never parted with a companion, yet my heart has been made to drink deep of the streams of afflictions by the loss of those that was very dear, but while we are receiving corrections from our Heavenly Father, may we learn obedience by the things we suffer. May our wills ever be in sweet subjection to the will of Him that always does all things well. May one thought give us consolation; that is the blessed hope of meeting our dear departed friends on the other side of Jordan, where sickness, pain and sorrow shall never come and parting sounds was never heard.

While I am writing, I can see in [my] imagination, my dear Nancy and Aurora [Clark] round the bed of their dying mother and can almost feel their heart rending pangs when her happy spirit took its flight from all earthly friends leaving the tenement of day to join the Heavenly host above to sing the praises of our dear earthly redeemer through a boundless eternity.

My heart rejoices to hear they have an interest in Christ and my sincere prayer is that they may ever adorn their [pro]fession by a well ordered life and Godly conversation. May pure religion be their Heavenly portion while passing through this world of sorrow and troubles and disappointments. That when their steps are numbered, they may die in the triumphs of a loving faith and meet their departed mother in the dimes of everlasting glory to enjoy her company forever.

Give my love to them; tell them to write. They would also write to Silas, [Carey] not forgetting poor Amanda [Miller Parker] and her dear little fatherless children. I am glad that one is a praying child. May he live long to comfort his mother, and may the rest be brought to the knowledge of the truth as it is in Jesus, for the promise is that He will be a father to the fatherless and the widow's God and guide.

I must now drop this subject and tell you [that] we are all in common health and all our connections, except brother Joseph [Lott]. He has been sick a long time with the chill and fever. He has been better and then worse. I have just heard he had another chill yesterday. I have not heard from him today.

Mother Lott is in unusual health though, very helpless. She sends her respects to you both. She was 82 years old the twelfth day of this month. Harriett [Trumbull] and Robert [Wells] has been very sick, but are some better. They send their love to you and sister Lydia, for they say my friends must be theirs.

It is a general time of health around us, but the cholera still rages in Columbus the last we heard, and that was lately. Many have left and come to Zoar and Delaware, and some to Sunbury [Ohio].

I expect by this time, you are impatient to hear from Thomas [Russell] [*Ed. note: Thomas Russell was the great-grandson of John Phillips; grandson of Mary Phillips and Isaac Hewitt; son of Lavina Hewitt and John Russell.*]

Well, I have good news to tell you. Last Sunday, they all arrived here well and hearty. Was in ... all the way. They called at Anson's [Williams]. Hannah [Phillips Williams] had been very sick, but was better. They told them to tell us nothing happened. They should be here this fall. We shall begin to look for them in about a week. They never told them anything about Cornwell [Phillips], so of course, we heard nothing from them.

Brother Ross and his wife wishes you to let their friends know that they are pleased with the country so far. They went out to their Uncle James [Osburn] last Tuesday and got back last night. They will write when they get settled. They expect to get a house near us this winter and look around before they buy.

You must tell John [Russell] and Lavina [Hewitt Russell] that Thomas [Russell] sends his love to them and Louis and Polly and Albert and little Sarah [Russell]. He would like to see them all, but he is not home sick, nor never has been. Sister Ross says he was a very good boy on the road nor never shed a tear the whole way. He has gone to meeting with his Uncle Henry. He appears some like our beloved Thomas that is gone. *[Ed. note: This is probably her son; there have been no records found to this date on Henry and Mary's family.]* We can't help but anticipate on some little comfort with him, but disappointments are so sure that I hope I shall be prepared to meet them.

I begun this letter last Sunday and shall finish it tonight, Wednesday. I have waited to see where brother Ross got a house. They have moved today, about one mile from here. He calculates to take a farm for a year or so. There was a man here last night, wants him to take one of his about a half mile from here. There is a great chance they can have as many apples as they want. I think he will take it, but can't say for certain, but will write soon and let their friends know all about it, but as they knew the folks would be anxious to hear from them, they wished me to write a few words for them as I expect you will let John and Lavina [Hewitt Russell] see it and they will inform them.

The fall has been middling seasonable. Their ... corn is poor. About here, potatoes is hardly middling and so is flax in general, though we [have a] very good crop of that. We have just heard the cholera has abated in Columbus.

My dear little Thomas [Russell] is yet well in a sweet sleep in the back room. Says he is not home sick and sends his best love to Grandfather and Grandmother. You must pardon the grey spots [of ink]; the letter must be finished tonight. For Thomas [Russell] and I are going to Sunbury tomorrow with brother Ross and his wife to get him a new hat, for he lost his on the way.

Henry sends love to you and sister Lydia in particular. Often says how I wish I could see them, but fear I never shall in this world. Oh, dear brother and sister, when you read this, can your hearts tell the feelings of mine, for this moment that doleful thought has again took possession and the sound is never, no, never, alas, never going to behold the faces of those I love so dear till this frail body shall return to its [original] dust, but be assured that through the merits of Him that died on the cross, I still feel a strong hope of meeting in heaven and enjoy your company forever.

Give my love to Mary [Goodrich Miller] when you see Stephen Miller and his; *[Ed. note: These are my 6th generation grandparents]* to Polly Felts and hers. I often think of them all, but can't anymore, for it is almost eleven o'clock. I am very tired and have some work that must be done before I lay the old carcass down to rest. I must say, accept my love, pardon the blunders, write soon. Farewell dear brother and sister and believe as now and forever, your unworthy, yet affectionate brother and sister,

Henry and Mary Lott

P. S. Samantha [Lott] sends her love to you and also to uncle should you see him. He did not write by Ross. She wants he should and put it in the Office; [Post Office] yours if convenient.

FAMILY OF JOHN RUSSELL

JOHN RUSSELL, b. 1794; d. 1851, Greenfield Township, Susquehanna PA, married about 1818, Lavina Hewitt, daughter of Isaac Hewitt and Mary Phillips, b. 22 January 1802; d. probably Greenfield Township, Susquehanna, PA.

CHILDREN

Had seven children; the following are recorded.

Lois, b. 1819, m. George Goodrich, d. 1899.

Albert, b. 1820 Greenfield Township, Susquehanna, PA; d. 1911.

Thomas, b. March 1824, Greenfield Township, Susquehanna, PA; d. 1891, m. Mercy White, Scott Township, Lackawanna, PA. Had 7 children.

Polly/ Mary Aurora, b. c. 1821, m. 1841 Lorenzo Parker Lavina Sarah, b. 1830, m. 1849 Eber White; d. 1853.

December 25, 1833

Dearest and Best Beloved Brother and Sister,

I have waited a long time for an answer to the letter I wrote one week after James Ross arrived here, but I have looked in vain. What can be the matter? I can not tell, but you know dear brother what is always my fears when I have to look longer than usual for a letter from you. [In] my fears sometimes, I [am] almost reduced to certainty that you or sister Lydia is very sick or dead.

That thought fills my mind while writing at this moment with heart rending pangs. Oh, is it possible that I shall never receive another letter from that dear hand that has so often soothed my sorrows and gave sweet consolation to my poor troubled breast. How oft have I thought; how can I have to look over the last line you will ever write to me, should I live to that period, sacred as it would be to me.

Yet the idea seems to chill the blood in all my veins and fill me with melancholy, but should this be the case, the same good Heavenly Father has promised to give strength equal to the day, and on His grace, I rely on his goodness. I depend through the merits of Jesus Christ our dear redeemer before all the ... of the Lord, where we shall never part; nor a sound of sickness, death or pain, one [never passes] our ears, but praises of God and the lamb shall be our employment through one eternal day.

I must now tell you, we are all in common health, except I am troubled with the toothache. The most of our friends and neighbors are in reasonable state of health, except brother Leonard's [Lott] daughter has lately been put to bed. I heard this morning, was very sick. She lives about four miles from here. Her father went up last night to see her. I expect him back tonight. We shall then hear from her. The roads arc so bad, it has been impossible for me to get there.

There has been two snows, but no sleighing. There has been no very cold weather, but I think we shall pay for it, before spring. We have got our flax roted and up. *[Ed. note: Roted is to soften the fibers of flax by soaking.]* We shall have about 200 weight. Our corn is very light and the fewest potatoes we have ever had since we kept house. But apples and peaches are very plenty. We have dryed so much as to be comfortable. The cow we took on share must be returned next

April. We shall have but one left. I have two heifers if they live. We hope they will come in a year from next spring. We must do the best we can until then.

I would be glad to write to John and Lavina Russell, but I must write Anson Williams or Cornwell [Phillips], for I have not seen nor heard a word from them since Rosses folks come, but tell them Thomas [Russell] is well contented. He has been to school and will go all winter. ... I have knit him a pair of mittens, made him new pantaloons, and going to make him another pair and a box coat, and then we are going to see his aunt Betsy Carpenter. Old Mr. Ross seen her. She told him, she meant to come and get him, but she had not been yet and she will not get him if she does come at [all[]; not till his father and mother come, or send particular orders.

We should like to know if John and Lavina has any thoughts of coming here next season. They know how glad we would be to see them. We also think and know if they was here, they would be better than they can there, for there is a greater chance for boot and shoe making and provision not so dear.

Tell James Ross folks, that they are all well. The old gentleman was here yesterday. He has been making our stairs and ceiling. They are yet [quite] pleased with the country and are like to do well if they have their health as they have had. Robert [Wells] is here. He sends his best respects to you. Harriett [Trumbull] and her husband and children are well. They all wish to be remembered.

And now, dear brother, if you are living and able to write, I do believe you will and let me know how you are and how the rest of my relatives are and if they ever think of poor old aunt Polly. I often think of them all and oft contemplate of the many visits I made while there, but oh, alas, solomn sensations fill my breast while ruminating on moments forever fled, never to return and I often think, oh, I shall never visit the land where I spent the days of my childhood and youth and where so many of my dear friends dwell and [if] I even go there, the places of some would be empty.

Poor Amanda [Miller Parker], how often I think of her and Silas [Clark]. Give my love to them. Let me know how they do and also Nancy and Aurora and Mary [Goodrich Miller] should [you] see her. I believe they will, none of them, even write. And also Polly P. Felts and Polly [Tripp] Millard and her family; James Tripp and his; Stephen Miller and his; Caleb's widow, Comer [Phillips] and his; Samuel Miller and his *[Ed. note: This* is *my grandfather, 7th generation]*. Let me hear from as many as you can find time and paper, but do let me know if John Miller has returned to his wife.

It is growing dark. I must close by sending our love and best wishes to you and believe us now and forever, your affectionate brother and sister.

Henry and Mary Lott

P. S. Excuse my blunders. It is dark and I can't look over them. Let me know if you have got your pension. Farewell.

CHAPTER V

I began this letter two weeks ago and have been trying to finish it ever since, but every day brought its cares and now, I must close it by candlelight.

February 2, 1834

My Dearest Brother and Sister,

I received your very welcome letter. I had waited a long time and sent to the Post Office many times expecting to find one, and as many times was disappointed and returned heavy hearted and had almost given up the idea of ever receiving any more from your dear hand. But, at last it came by the hand of my dear friend Robert Wells. He heard it was to the Post Office, went, paid his own money, got it and brought it to me.

The feelings of my heart I shall not attempt to describe, when breaking the seal. My poor heart rejoiced to hear you was both in the land of the living and although I must never entertain the least hopes of ever seeing your faces on this side of the grave or clasping you again to this fond bosom, yet the chilling thought of never receiving another letter from them I hold so dear, it is almost too much for me at times to be reconciled to.

I wish to be in subjection to our Heavenly Father and although we are separated in body, yet I often think, and these thoughts afford me sweet consolation particular at night when all others are locked in the arms of sleep, that we are not only bound by the ties of natural affection, but our hearts are double united by those strong ties of Heavenly union that death itself, I trust and believe will not be able to dissolve.

And when these eyes have let fall a few more tears, when these hearts have heaved a few more sighs, when a few more sorrows have passed by, a few more afflictions endured, we shall meet on the other side of Jordan in that fair haven of everlasting rest, and recount our suffering and with all our friends that have gone before together with all the [mercy] of the Lord where we shall need no sun by day, nor moon to give light by night, but the presence of the Lamb shall be light through eternal day. We shall forever behold His glory without a dimming veil between, and in sweet anthems in songs of redeeming grace ..., so we sing Glory, Glory to the lamb that died to redeem us to Him. Be Glory forever, Amen.

I must now drop this heart cheering subject and tell you, we are all in common state of health at present. Thomas is yet afflicted with his eyes, but does some work. He is now dressing flax. We had a very good crop last year. Henry and I have been preparing for making sugar. We have made 25 pounds, but when we shall make anymore is very uncertain, for it has been very warm for several days and no appearance of cold at present.

We had but little cold weather this winter. Some snow, but scarcely any sleighing. It has been health this winter till of late. Henry and I went last night to see Jedidiah Taylor about two miles from here. He lies very low with a fever. They told us that the doctor said there was a number very sick in Renksh and some other places.

Mother Lott is yet living, though almost helpless. She can't bare the weight on her feet, and [is] almost senseless. We think she cannot stay much longer. James Ross' folks are well a few days ago and doing well. They have bought 45 acres of good land with a small improvement, gave [them] their wagon and horses and took a deed. It is thought they made a great bargain. We think their friends have heard from them before this time, for they have wrote three and have long been looking for one from them. I shall expect to hear from them all when they get their letters, for they write for me and I for them, and shall expect you and them to do the same that we may all hear the oftener from each other.

I have not heard a word from Anson [Williams] or Cornwell [Phillips] since I wrote last. Tell John [Russell] and Lavina [Hewitt] that Thomas [Russell] is well and well contented, But I am very sorry to say he is not the child we expected, but we hope and think he will make a smart man when he gets over some bad tricks that I forbear naming at present. We hope John and Lavina [Russell] will come and see us this season.

His Aunt Betsy Carpenter wants him very much and we think he would do better there than here, for we had a boy of five years old that we took from town and as he is bound, we must of course, keep him. *[Ed. note: There is no record in Delaware Co. court records of an apprenticeship. It is possible that they could have taken him in without documentation, or the document was lost or recorded elsewhere.]*

Was Thomas [Russell] like his Uncle Thomas, they could do well enough, for he is a very pleasant disposition child and appears to love Thomas as he does his eyes, but it grieves me to say it is very different with Thomas [Russell]. But we shall keep him and do as well by him as we can till his father comes, or sends orders. He sends his love to all of you. Sometimes if asked, [he] says he would like to see his brother and sisters.

I begun this letter the 2nd day thinking to have sent it by mail, but have seen Robert Cartherton. Since he told me he was going with a drove of horses to Jersey and should go through Masonville and it is possible he would take it where you would get it. Harriett [Trumbull] and family are well, send their Love to you. Robert [Wells] is now waiting to direct and take the letters to the Post Office. He sends his best respects to you.

It is most meeting time and I must omit some things I would have wrote, for I should have wrote finer had I not been in such haste, but dear sister Lydia, how oft I think of you, and oft think how much comfort we took, oh could I but have you to go to meeting with me today. What would I give, but it can not be, no, we meet no more till we meet in Heaven.

My love to Silas [Clark] and his children, to Amanda and hers, to all your children and grandchildren, to Elder Miller and all the friends of Jesus. Let me hear from Silas Carey and his mother, wish he would write to me. Do let me hear from cousin Bates, and now my dear brother and beloved sister, I must draw to a close. Henry and Thomas join with me in love to you. I remain your affectionate sister, farewell.

Henry and Mary Lott

July 20, 1834

My Ever Dear Brother and Sister,

In the midst of sickness and trouble, I have sit down a few moments to inform you of our present situation, and in hopes of receiving a few lines from your dear hand once more for a consolation to this poor afflicted heart that has so long been a seat of trouble, pain and sorrow.

One week ago today, I closed a letter to my dear Tryphena [Hewitt Lee] in answer to one I received from her, that gave me the account of the death of her dear babe. Poor girl, I think my heart knows something of the feelings of hers, but I rejoice that her confidence is still unshaken, and in the hour of greatest trouble, she has a friend to go to even; Jesus whose soft hand will soon wipe away the tears from all His dear children and take them home to Himself. I told her to send her letter to you that you might hear from us for it seemed then as though I could hardly ever get a chance to write to you, but as it is some distance I fear you will not get it soon and I am anxious to hear from you.

I thought I would try to write at least a few lines. Four weeks today, Thomas was taken very unwell, but kept about till Tuesday. He was then taken intimately down and has remained so ever since. I doctored and nursed [him] till Friday. We then sent for a doctor. Since that, we have called the neighbors twice, supposing he was dying. [He] has a very bad cold that seems impossible to cure. Has had a high fever and still has some at times. He also has a wonderful break in his privates and groans a great part of the time with a pain in his side and back. He grows poor and finely, he is not much more than a skeleton now.

I have never had a night's rest since he was taken. I have had a girl one week, but Henry thinks we are not able to hire and I must do alone except my two little boys for I had to send for Thomas Russell home to help me. He was boarding with an old lady and going to school. He is well and appears contented. He is now gone to meeting.

Give our love to John and Lavina [Russell] and Polly. Tell them I should be glad to get a line from them, but I can't write particular to them, as I wish, nor indeed to none of you, for Thomas is wanting me every few minutes. My letter will be very unconnected, but I expect you will find it out, understand it, and pardon all blunders. I solicit your prayers dear brother and sister, and not out of complements, but because I really stand in great need of them, for I feel I want daily grace and although I have long been accustomed to wear the yoke, and long been to the school of affliction, yet I have learned but little of the pure wisdom that comes from above.

Very sensible I am that in my present situation I need much of the grace of God, much Christian fortitude, and much patience to do right, for as a friend and joy, Henry is much out of patience to think it must take me nearly all my time to do my housework and take care of Thomas. He is much less trouble then I should expect for one in his situation, and as sick as he has been and finely still is, I wait on him very freely and shall as long as duty calls. Although I feel almost wore out, yet, where I shall be given equal to the day was it Henry that lay sick, it would be very different in some respects.

For there are some of our neighbors that think I take more pains with him than I need, particular in keeping him clean, but I thank the Lord for a principle that makes me believe that he ought to be kept as clean [as] the Governor, and has given me health and strength thus far to do so. I have washed every day but three since he was taken and changed him and his bed every day, but we do think if his cough would wear off, he might get along, but if it should prove to be the consumption, how long he may stay, we know not, but we all know the consequences of such complaints.

It is almost night and I have a thousand things I want to write. I will say I have not heard a word from Anson [Williams] or Cornwell [Phillips] since I told you. I guess they have forgot us all, but I shall write to them soon. Mother Lott is failing. Samantha and her family are well. She sends her love and [to] her Uncle David Silsbee. She would like to hear from him. Brother Leonard and his are in common health. His home ever is ...

Poor Carney's folks are well. Ross' folks are pretty well. She will lay abed in ... this month, Thomas went to visit them Thursday and come home Friday. Rosencranse's people are all common health. Esquire Daniel [Rosencranse] has never returned and we expect never will. If I could see [you] I could tell you all about it.

My dear Harriett [Trumbull] has moved about ... miles from me. Her health is always poor. The rest of her family is well. She and her husband and children was all here three weeks ago today, one of the times when we thought Thomas was dying. She always sends her love to you. Robert [Wells] was here two weeks ago. He is well and doing well. He is teaching school about twelve miles from here toward Newark [Ohio].

There was a great deal of damage done by the floods ... since there was a doctor ... twelve miles from here, and on the Ohio River, there was a number of sheep, some hogs and one or two horses. We have heard of it, the greatest freeze that was ever known in these parts. Likewise, it was the coldest spring that ever was known here. The frost killed all the fruit, even the crab apples and plums, so we are all on an average in regard to that. We thought one spell we should have no wheat, but some has pretty good crops. We shall have but little; folks are in the height of harvest. Do let us know how the season and crops are with you.

My love to Silas Clark and Nancy and Aurora; Polly Millard and her family; poor Amanda [Miller Parker] and hers. Pray, let me know how they all are and how they get along. I have never received a letter from Silas Carey yet. Do let me know how he and his mother are and where they live. If you have heard from Francis [Phillips], do let me know. Give my love to all your children and grandchildren and great-grand children that you see, and all others inquiring friends if any there be and accept the same yourselves. Oh, that I could but see you once more, but why have I wrote them words when I know it can never be below the sun? No, no, that thought is like a dagger to my poor heart to meet you no more on earth, but one sweet thought still remains that gives life to my Lord is, soon I shall meet them in Heaven, no more to part or farewell.

I remain your affectionate sister,

Mary Lott

P.S. I forgot to tell you crops of corn look well and flax is middling.

August and September 1834

My Dearest and Surely Best Beloved Brother and Sister,

I have once more sit down to write you, and first will tell you we received your kind, welcome letter three weeks ago. I should have answered it immediately, but I had sent one about two weeks before. For I have waited with much impatience, and been, or sent as often, to the Post Office as [I had been] expecting an answer to one sent by Rufus Atherton. He told me when he returned, he left it at Razorville, but appears you never got it, but if you have got the last I sent, you will be anxious to hear from us again by the time this gets there.

When I wrote, I had no reason to think Thomas would be alive now, but he still continues and sometimes he seems some better and then worse. His cough is not so hard. He raises a great deal of bad smelling matter, has had a [good] appetite for some time, but gains no flesh. What will be the end of his sickness, God only knows, but I know He will do all things well. You will guess something of my feelings when I tell you, I have not had a night's rest, since he was taken. Two nights and one day I was very sick. I never sat up, nor scarce done a chore.

Yesterday, I went to see poor old Mother Lott that is helpless and almost senseless, though [she] has often inquired why Polly did not come. I had been there about an hour when I was taken in great distress. I had hard work to get home, but I am better today and what has helped me [is] James Ross and his wife has been here. She has also been confined. I have not seen her in a long time. She has got a fine son; calls it Ziba. They are all in common health. It is dark. I must finish in the morning.

I am very unwell this morning, but hope to be better soon. Thomas is much the same. Dear brother and sister, I think of you as much as you can of me, and oh, could I but have the privilege of conversing with you personally instead of writing, how it would sooth my poor throbbing breast. I could tell you some of the trials I have passed through for nine weeks. And in your friendly arms for a moment, forget my pain, but also it can never be, no, that can never be and I submit to the will of my Heavenly Father, fully believing that my pilgrimage will, ere a great while as well as yours, come to an end.

I do expect that through the merits of a once crucified, but now risen Savior, we shall meet in that happy land where the inhabitants shall not say; I am sick. Where we shall be swallowed up in love. Oh yes, there we shall meet our departed friends, together with all the ransomed of the Lord, and no thoughts of parting once interrupt our joys. Till that period, let us be patient. And do, dear brother and sister, pray for me, that my afflictions may be more weaned from earthly objects, and that I may bear many afflictions that yet await me, with Christian fortitude and perfect resignation, for I well know, I need much grace, much humility, to bear up under my present situation, but my trust is in God who is able and I believe yet, will bring me ... conquer and land me safe on the other side of Jordan.

I wrote to Anson [Williams] and Cornwell [Phillips] a week after I did you. When shall I get an answer I cannot say, but I will let you know if I ever do. My health is about as usual, but I really feel almost wore out. Samantha Lott sends her love to you, thanks for writing about her uncle David and wishes you would let her know again.

It is a week since I began this letter and it has seemed almost impossible to find time to finish it amidst so many cares and so much work as there is every day for poor me, but can tell you that Thomas is considerable better than he was last Sunday. He can walk out occasionally. If he gets no [fever] back, I think he will get along. His sickness has come pretty hard on me, but I feel no disposition to complain. I have pretty much all my wool to spin and besides some weaving I owe and have promised for others.

Thomas Russell has commenced going to school again and boards with the same old lady. He is here now and is well. I know of few that is very sick, but a number complaining. The colary [cholera] is in Newark and very bad on the Sandusky and also at Portland and Cleveland.

James Ross' brother Samuel, come here about five weeks ago. He has been to the Rocky Mountains, since that to England. Has come and set up a blacksmith shop one mile from here. Appears to be smart and very steady. It has been a long time since I heard from Stephen Gautier. Do let me know how and where they are and don't forget to let me know where Silas Carey and his mother is, and also how Amzi Wilson's wife is.

And Polly Felts and her family; give my love and best wishes to them all, and Silas Clark and poor Amanda Parker. I often think of them and would like to know how they get along, and also Caleb Miller's widow and family; and Polly Millard and her family; and Pamelia [Tripp] and hers; and John Russell and Lavina and their children. Let me know if he has heard from his father.

I can't name them all, but I must say Samuel and Susannah Miller, and Comer [Phillips] and his wife, and my dear little Hannah [Phillips]. Let me know if you have got your pension. I wrote in my last letter about the season, I shall but just say, the summer crops are pretty good in general.

Dear brother, can you imagine the feelings of my poor heart when I read your dream, for about the same time, I dreamed of seeing you and I thought that you had to go and I knew I should never see you again in this world. I awaked crying and thought you was surely gone and I should never get another letter from your dear hand, but I have one more and hope for the best.

Samuel Ross has just come in. He says you must not tell his folks that he was here till Brittain's had started here, for he wants to take them on surprise. I have not seen my dear Harriett [Trumbull] in nine weeks. Her husband was here a few days ago; said her health is very poor. Robert [Wells] is yet at Johnstown, his school is nearly out. They always say give my love to your dear brother. Henry and I often talk about you. He sends his love to you and all your friends.

Thomas and little Tommy [Russell] send their love to all. Give my love to Fanny [Phillips]. Tell her, she must not get tired of waiting on you and Lydia, for I know she will get well rewarded in this world and that indeed to come. I must close. Accept my love and believe me now and forever, your affectionate sister.

Mary Lott

November 1834

My Dearest and Truly Best Beloved Brother and Sister,

Once more, I lift my pen to let you know that through the mercy of Him that never sleeps nor slumbers, we are all alive and in common health. Thomas has got well and appears in common health, is full [and is] as hearty as in several years and we sincerely hope that this will find you and yours enjoying good health.

We received your welcome letter night before last, but dear brother and sister, I shall not attempt to describe the feelings of my poor heart when my eye caught the sight of a letter written by your dear hand and I do feel thankful to our Heavenly Father for all His loving kindness to me a poor, unworthy worm of the dust and particular for preserving your life so long, for although we are separated by many a long mile and rugged mountains, vales, and rivers, must fear divide out mortal bodies? Yet how soothing is the Heaven born ties of friendship even when conveyed through the medium of the Post Office and this privilege dear brother [makes] esteemable all earthly treasures, but while writing a thought just struck my mind, oh, could I but see them once more and once more press them to this fond bosom, and oh, once more hear the sound of those sweet voices that has so often cheered my drooping spirits, but alas my anxieties are vain and I must submit to Him that always does all things well.

I must now tell you that we have had a visit from Anson [Williams] and Hannah [Phillips Williams] and their youngest child, dear little Rebecca, about four years old. They came to Buffalo [New Yor] in the stage, then in the steamboat to Cleveland [Ohio], then in the canal to Newark [Ohio]. Then he hired a stage to bring them to our house. He gave nine dollars to the man that brought them. They stayed a week here and to his brother [John Williams] that lives twelve miles from here. *[Ed. note: John lived in Sunbury and is on the 1820 Delaware County census.]*

Henry and I went with them there, stayed two nights. They stayed two nights longer, then his brother and son and his wife came with them. Anson and his brother went to see another of his sons about fifteen miles another way, and next day, he and his wife came and stayed from Friday till Sunday. Then Henry and I went with them to Sunbury, stayed all night. Monday, about two o'clock, we took the parting hand and we heard that soon after, they took the stage for home. We have not heard from them yet, but they promised to write or ... Cornwell [Phillips].

They say he is doing pretty well. He lives on Anson's farm though Deborah [Doud Phillips] has been very sick a long time. They thought she would not live, but was much better. Anson liked the country very much. He has agreed for one thousand acres of land three miles beyond his brother's, but said he did not know whether he should even come, but wanted it for his children. I expect he has five sons-in-law by this time. They expected his five daughters to be married as soon as they returned. *[Ed. note: Anson did move to Ohio and created a town called Williamsville; see plat map, page 89.]*

Sister Elizabeth [Lott] is entirely blind and her health has been very poor a long time. She lives with her daughter, but had been to Anson's on a visit four or five weeks and had just gone home. Hannah told me to tell you when I wrote, that she had not forgot you. She tried to have Anson and Cornwell write to you, but I expect Cornwell has to work every moment out of necessity and Anson is so rich and so much to attend to, that he can't spend time to write to any one. You will understand that I don't say this to apologize for either of them.

We have had also a visit from Henry's brother's wife that lives in York State twelve miles from Ithaca between the lakes [Seneca County]. They had been gone a week when Anson come. We have had a real time of visiting this fall, but amongst them all, I could not see my dearest and best beloved brother and sister. No, that can't be, but I must not let these feelings over balance my judgement or I can't finish my letter tonight and I meant to send it to Sunbury tomorrow morning by Robert Wells. [He] is here and sends his best respects.

Your poor Harriett [Trumbull], I have not seen her but once since last June. She is now confined at home with a sick child that has been sick nearly all summer and grows worse. I can't go to see her for I can't leave home all night and besides, Thomas being sick almost all summer has put me so back with my work, that I must not spend any time going about unless it is a case of death. 1 have not got any wool hardly half clipped and but a short piece wove, hardly enough to make us comfortable, but I have more almost ready to weave. When I weave [it will be] a short piece to pay for things I had when Thomas was sick.

You wrote about the preacher that has made so much divisions in churches. I have heard some little concerning him. I should like to know his name and if you have seen him. I have always been a friend to missionary societies and am no enemy yet, but I wish you would read the first chapter of Colossians : 23 verse and tell me if you think that Paul meant that Christ's commission that he gave to his disciples was fulfilled when he says "the hope of the Gospel which ye have heard and which was preached to every creature which is under Heaven whereof I, Paul, am made a minister," for I confess I do not fairly understand it.

I began this letter two weeks ago and have been trying to finish it ever since, but every day brought its cares and now, I must close it by candlelight. I fear you will be plagued to find it out, for I have not thought I could write by candlelight for a long time.

Thomas Russell is well and will commence going to school next week if he gets his new shoes as we expect. It has been fine weather all the fall till eleven days ago. Since then, it has been raining, but not cold till last night. It snowed a little for the first time and tonight it is pretty cold. Today is the 23rd of November.

John Ross was here. After he came, I told him I must send some letters by him. He said he should be here again; the next we heard, he was gone. Don't fail of writing soon, for I hardly know how to wait and want to hear how sister Lydia stood her visit to Salomn [Wayne Co. Pennsylvania]. And how our dear Mary [is] and all her children, and why Tryphena [Hewitt Lee] has not answered my letter. Give my love to them should you *see* them and accept the same yourselves.

Samantha Lott's mother lives with her. She went from here last Tuesday, stayed with us a week. She sends her love to you. A letter to her brother [David Silsbee] will go in with mine. It is now eleven o'clock. Farewell dear brother and sister. Believe me now and forever, your loving sister.

Henry and Mary Lott

CHAPTER VI

If you come, we shall receive you heartily with open hearts and arms, but if you choose to stay amongst the mountains, rocks and stones, you must. I have no more to say.

August 1835

Dear Brother,

Once more, I sit down to write a few lines to let you know we are yet alive for which we feel thankful to our Heavenly Father, and we sincerely hope these lines and the berry will find you and yours in good health as can be expected for people of your age. I have not time to write but little at this time, but will tell you that old Mr. Wilcox's grand- daughter Betsy, now James Stark's wife, I expect will start for Pennsylvania tomorrow or next day.

She has promised to go to see you and she will tell you more than I could write had I ever so much time. And brother Joseph Lott and his wife, and brother Leonard [Lott] is preparing to go as soon as possible. Samantha [Lott] has just gone to see her Uncle David [Silsbee]. I shall then write again. If I am alive and well, we begin to look for an answer to the one I sent by John Carney. We have received the one you wrote in answer to the one I wrote to Solomon Millard.

We was very glad to hear you was yet alive, but sorry to hear your afflictions with sore eyes and mouth, but hope they are well by this time. I think it will be the best for Solomon Millard to move here, but I dare not urge him to come for fear he might not like it and then he would blame me. But, I often think of them poor fellows that are digging away among the rocks and stones and may I not say hills, and then think how many hundred acres there is here unoccupied that is level, rich, and some so loose you can kick it up as you walk along. I often wish they could have enough if no more of Ohio soil for a good large garden spot, but however, I can't take it to them, they must come to it or some other country or dig there all their lives.

Perhaps, now he would like to know the inconveniences. There are some. I will assure you for not withstanding, there is so much good land it will not produce without hard labor. It is generally pretty heavy timbered and folks have to work hard till they get it cleared up and then they can live pretty easy, at least I know some that does and there is something more, sometimes a creature dies with the murrain [*Ed. note: any of a variety of infectious diseases of cattle.]* and sometimes people sicken and die and some of the water has to be broke as we call it with lye, but everybody can have rain troughs and catch water, and rain water will wash as good here as anywhere. Sometimes, we think we don't have rain enough and sometimes we think we have too much, but however, I think summer crops in general will be pretty good and flax is very good.

John Brittain was here today, says his folks, James Ross and Kimbles were all in common health and we think thay are doing pretty well. It is most night and must carry my letter to brother Stark. I shall soon have to close, but my dearest brother and sister, how can I have the thought of never seeing your faces more, or clasping you to this fond bosom, but oh dear, I suppose it must be so. Well, the will of God be done in this and all things else, but be assured, I still expect by the grace of God to meet you in the upper and far better world, where we shall see as we are seen, and know as we are known, and our love and Heaven born ties of affection shall be renewed, and we shall part no more, but shall sing praises to God and the Lamb through one eternal day.

Give my love to my dear Fanny. Tell her I shall ever love her for her being good to you. Tell Silas Clark I often think of him and poor Amanda [Miller Parker]. Have [you] seen or heard from Silas Carey? Do let me know. I would say more to your children, grand-children and great grand-children; time and paper fails, but give my love and best wishes to them all. Tell them not to forget me. Henry and I and all the rest join with me in love to you. And now believe, in your affectionate sister till death dissolves these earthly frames and joins us in Heaven above in prospect of that blessed hour. I once more say farewell.

Henry and Mary Lott

April 21, 1836

My Dearest and Well Beloved Brother and Sister,

I received two letters from you, and one from James and David Tripp all the same time, [in] two days. I had been waiting a long time and had about concluded you was very sick or dead. Dear brother, I trembled when I asked for them at the Post Office, but how did my heart leap with joy when I see your hand writing. How glad was I to hear you was alive and in usual health, but poor Amzi Wilson's wife, she is gone. Well, I hope to meet her on the fair banks of final deliverance when the storm of this short life is past. [*Ed. note: Phelena Wetherby died January 12, 1835*]

I will now tell you, we are all in common health except poor Thomas. He has laid confined to his bed all winter and remains yet. We hope when warm weather comes he will get as to walk again, for he has not walked a step since some time in January. James and David Tripp wrote that they and Solomon A. Millard talked of moving to this country this season and wished me to describe the winters and the summers and prices of stock provisions, but we thought best to write all that I can write at this time in this one letter here. You send it to them as soon as possible, but first I will say as I said in my other, I would rather never see one of my relatives than have them play James Ross and John Brittain. I therefore shall never urge none of them to come for fear they will get homesick for the good old Pennsylvania mountains and rocks and stones and then blame me, for be assured they will find none of them here.

I will tell them what they will be sure to find if they go in the woods. Some good sturdy birches, some hickory, some black walnuts, and them pretty good size, and some tall straight oaks and some of the largest they ever saw, and many beautiful maples affords our sugar and molasses. Some buck eyes, some paupaus [*Ed. note; I have been unable to determine if this is an old name or if the name was incorrectly spelled.*] The underbrush is chiefly dogwood, nonnas, and a great deal of spice bush, and now if they calculate to go in the woods, they expect to find some pretty hard work, before they get a farm cleared. There must none expect to come to Ohio and get a living without hard work, unless they are able to buy improved farms or have a pocket full of money as Anson Williams is.

I will now describe the last winter as near as my memory will serve. We have had the coldest winter that ever was known in these parts. Cold weather set in some time in November, continued till the last of March, but we had not snow enough to cover the ground, till towards the last of February. It fell about one half a foot deep in about a week. There fell near half as much more, but the first was nearly gone when the next fell, and it was off by the middle of March, but there has been some warm spells all winter so that some had made two hundred weight of sugar by March, but we did not begin till the first of April.

We have made 150 weight of sugar, seven gallons of molasses sugar, ... pound molasses; 75 cents per gallon, ... dollars per bushel, but there is enough ... Corn has been 37 cents but is now 31 cents; oats has been 25 cents, but is now 20 cents per bushel. Pork last fall was three dollars and a half a hundred. It is now 8 cents per pound. Butter from 1 to 12 cents per pound. Cows from 12 to 15 dollars; a good yoke of cattle from 50 to 60 [dollars], perhaps some less and some more. Sheep in the spring from 2 to 3 dollars; hay aplenty yet for 3 dollars per ton; potatoes 25 cents a bushel. All these things higher than they ever was before, but be assured there is plenty in the country and can be had for labor. Flax, 8 cents per pound. People have been plowing more than a week and some have made good gardens, though I think it is too soon, for it has rained and thundered today and I fear we shall have some frost yet for it is some cool.

Perhaps James Ross will get there before the letter will for they started last Monday. We heard they got two miles and a half the first day. How they have got along since, we don't know. Henry and I went to see them the day before they started. They talked some of going up somewhere toward the head of the Allegheny. They had heard of a great tract of land, but Henry told them he had explored that part of the country when young, and told them if they would give him all the land there he would not take it as a precious gift, but however, we have no thought they will make any stop except what they are obliged to till they reach Abington, and we believe James in particular will strive harder to get there then the children of Israel did from the promised land. They started the worst time they could, took the worst road they could find. What stories they will tell we don't know and finely, I don't know as it matters as much for them that would be discouraged for tales they hear from them that had as good a home as James Ross had and leave it would never have courage enough to come to Ohio or any other place.

And now I have told you the truth. If you come, we shall receive you heartily with open hearts and arms, but if you choose to stay amongst the mountains, rocks, and stones, you must. I have no more to say. Only Mr. Kimble after he sold his place took in his brain, took a farm in Bennington [Ohio] about five miles from here. I see them all yesterday in Sunbury. They were well except their youngest daughter had been unwell.

Some days old Mr. Ross was here ... went away. I read my letters to him, ... most crazy particular about Esen..., next day after they started. [I] did not see them for which I was very sorry, but I think I will stop writing about [them], only wish them good luck on their journey to the promised land, hoping if they ever return to this poor country again, they will try to content themselves and know when they are well off.

Dear brother, I often think of you and oft recall past happiness, but to dwell on pleasures gone by to be recalled no more is but momentary consolation, for that mournful thought still occupies my mind, never, no never, no more, shall I clasp you to this fond bosom, no more shall I sit by your friendly fire side in sweet conversation. You wished it could be so that I could come see you once more. Alas, that would be more pleasure than I ever hope to enjoy, yet it is not impossible, but at least I will sometime almost indulge hope of seeing you again in this life, but if not, I shall have strong faith that I shall meet you in Heaven, no more to part, forever.

Anson [Williams] and Hannah [Phillips Williams] was here last week. Stayed one night. They have moved in his son and son-in-law. They started the 23rd day, arrived to his brother's the 17th day, a week ago last Saturday night all well. I expect them here again next week.

Thomas Russell is well, has lately made his Aunt Betsy Carpenter a week's visit. They want him to come to live with them till of age. I told him to tell them if they would write to his father and he wished him to he might go. If not, and his father wants him home, we will send him the first good chance. They say he must come and go to school this summer, and when I get his summer clothes made I shall let him go a spell at least. If you see any of John's folks [John Russell], give my love to them. Tell them not to be uneasy about him, for I will assure them, he shall be well taken care of.

If you see Silas Carey, do give my love to him and remind him of his promise. If I had not so many cares on my mind and so much to do, Thomas being sick all winter and like to remain so, I would write him another letter, and I think I shall before long and see if I can't get one from him whom I feel so strongly bound to by the thoughts of childhood.

Mother Lott is living, tho helpless and almost senseless. I read my letter to Samantha [Lott] and her mother. They are well and thank you for letting them hear from David Silsbee, send their love to you and hope you will write again. Esther Williams went from here today. I wrote a letter for her to send to her son, Jonathon Jenkins that moved to Illinois last fall. Her father, old Uncle John Williams is yet alive though very feeble. He is 94 years if he lives till next March.

Salt is $2.50 a barrel, wild land is from $2-$3. Congress land is to be one dollar per acre after the fourth of July. Improvements come higher. I can't let the price, but if you could light of some more James Rosses and John Brittains, you might get them pretty cheap. *[Ed. note: Mary is using the archaic meanings of "let" to replace and "light" to happen upon.]*

My dear Mary [Phillips Hewitt], I get no letters from her or Isaac. What can be the reason? Have they forgot me or can't they write well? Give my love to them. My dear Fanny, I hope you are with your dear old grandfather and grandmother. Your grandfather says you are a good girl. Well, I hope you will always continue to be so. I shall always love you. Give my love to Polly Millard, to James Tripp's wife and David's [Tripp] wife. Tell them, if they start for Ohio, they must bid mountains and deep snows farewell and keep good courage on the way. Henry, Abigail, Thomas Russell all join in love with me. *[Ed. note: Abigail may be Henry's niece.]*

I remain your affectionate sister, Mary Lott

Plat of Williamsville

July 10, 1836

Dear and Best Beloved Brother and Sister,

I have waited a long time in hopes [of] receiving a letter from you, but get none. I fear you are sick or dead. I feel as tho I must write a few lines, fully believing I shall get an answer to this soon from some of you. I must now inform you of our situation, which is not very prosperous at this time. Brother Thomas is yet confined, can't walk a step.

Three weeks ago yesterday Henry and I started in a one horse wagon to go to Anson's [Williams]. Got in five miles of there. The horse fell to kicking and ran away, broke one bone of [Henry's] left leg, but I stuck to the hind part of the wagon till he ran near a quarter of a mile. It then struck a hog pen and it upset. I sprung and cleared it without being hurt any. The wagon stove all to pieces. The horse ran to the next house and the man stopped him. The folks was very kind to us, got word to Anson. The next morning he come with a wagon and would take us to his house and we found them all in common health.

Hannah [Phillips Williams] talked about you, wished me to remember her best love to you and sister Lydia. We stayed till Tuesday. Then, Sanford and little John brought us home. Henry begins to go on some crutches, but we fear he will not be able to do a great deal through haying and harvest. Our wheat looks well and wheat in general appears good. Some com looks very well, some middling, hay is very good.

Tell James Ross the wheat he left is very good. We should like to hear from them and know how he likes the country. We heard they landed safe at Ball Mountain and that is all we heard. The old gentleman Ross was here the other day. He lives with Sam ... He is well. He wishes you would try to let them know how anxious he is to have some of them write. He says he thinks John's wife Nancy will write if none of the rest do.

We want to hear from James and David Tripp and Solomon Millard. We fear that Ross and Brittain has told them such a lamentable story, it has discouraged their ever coming, but I hope not, for I think it would be so much better for them and their children, yet

I dare not urge, but tell them if they was here now, they could get wheat for 75 cents per bushel, corn for 25 cents, young potatoes, and other source plenty.

Mr. Kimble's folks are well, that is leaving. I expect you have heard their misfortune of losing their daughters. Thomas Russell went there last Saturday to visit them. If you see any of John Russell's folks, give them our best love. Tell them, we are the same. They need not be concerned about him. He is well and appears contented and be assured, we shall do as well by him as our circumstances will admit. We sent him to his Aunt Betsy Carpenter's to go to school. She had wanted him to come. He stayed ten days, but did not go a day, nor did they give him the least present, so we thought we would keep him to home and let him go here, but our teacher was taken sick and about that time, Henry broke his leg and we wanted him to help us, but mean he shall go all we can have a chance.

Poor John and Lavina, I feel sorry for them. I often think of them and think if they was here, they could do better, for he could [buy] provisions much cheaper than he can there. I began this letter a week ago. Have waited in hopes of getting one from you, but in vain. This morning, I must close it and send it. What can be the matter? Are you sick or dead? Oh, I can't bear the thought that you are gone, that I shall hear from you no more. Well, if you are living, I know you will write when you get this. I would inform you that we are all well, yet in common health.

Henry's leg has got so he hobbles about, has mowed some grass, cut some wheat, but his foot and leg swells when he walks on it and I fear it never will be well again, being obliged to go on it [so] soon, but we will hope for the best. Mother Lott is living, but she is helpless and senseless. Samantha and her mother is well and send their love to you. Would like to hear from David Silsbee. Our connections are in common health.

I heard from old Mr. John Williams yesterday. He has been very feeble all summer. Poor old man, his glass is almost run out, he is 93 or 94 years. He wants to see me very much. I have the thought I would go, but I am very much confined, it seems almost impossible for me to get away from home a night and I can't go and come in one day.

I still follow weaving for other folks. I have thought I would quit weaving [for] any one but ourselves, but necessity will still drive me, but I think I shall have to stop before long for I feel I fail faster and faster every year; the second day of next month 57 years have passed over my head should I live till that time. And dear brother and sister, my anxiety to see you once more is beyond description, but I must try to be reconciled to the will of Heaven. [*Ed. note: The writing on the original was apparently illegible because Hildah Brown has indicated Mary's age as 52, 54, or 57. On the 1840 census, she* is *shown between 50 - 60 years old.*]

I often dream of you and imagine I clasp you to this fond bosom, but alas when I awake it is but a dream and distance still divides me from those I so dearly love, but one bright hope still gladdens my soul; that is the storm of life will soon be past when you and 1 shall meet at last, where we shall enjoy each other's company and even range those blissful fields of glory, and not a thought of parting once interrupt our joy. Give my best love to your children, grandchildren, and great grandchildren and all the other inquiring friends. Accept the same yourselves and believe me now and forever, your affectionate sister. Farewell at present. I shall write again soon.

Henry and Mary Lott

P.S. Let me hear from Silas Carey. I have no letters yet; and [none from] his mother.

CHAPTER VII

I was in hopes of seeing some of my relatives when I read your letter, but have looked till I have given up all hopes.

February 12, 1837

My Dearest and Best Beloved Brother and Sister,

After a long time, I once more sit down to write you and let you know we are yet alive, while some of our friends, since I wrote last, are now numbered with the pale nations of the dead. Mother Lott died the 7th December [1836]. We perceived no particular alteration but a few days before she died. Old Mr. John Williams was buried a week ago last Friday. I never heard of it till he was buried. I had calculated all winter to go and make him a visit, but many things has been to prevent me from that, as well as not answering your last letter which I received in fifteen days after date. *[Ed. note: John Williams died February 2, 1837, and is buried in Sunbury Memorial Park, Sunbury, Delaware County, Ohio].*

Samantha's [Lott] mother had then laid very sick some time, that none that see her thought she would live, and by the time she got a little better, Samantha was taken. She has not been able to sit up five minutes in five weeks. She is in the term of life and her life has almost run away, and I have had to be there a great deal of my time, for some things she thinks none can do for her but me.

I come from there yesterday. We was in hopes she was rather on the mend, but she has a bad cough and can't say what it will terminate in, but hope for the best. Her mother has got so to be about [the] house, but not well. They both send their love and best wishes to you and thank you for writing to them, and wish you to let David Silsbee hear from them, and send their love to him and want he should write, for they have got no letter from him yet.

I was to Mr. Kimbles about three weeks ago. They were all well, but had got no letter from ... nor none of the rest. They wonder what can be the reason. We often get together and talk about you all and read your letters, and sometimes in imagination, we are almost with you. When you write again, let me know [how] James Ross' wife has been and how her boy is with his sore foot and how they are doing.

Give my love and best wishes to her. Tell her when Mrs. Kimble and I get together, we sit up almost all night to talk about her.

We should like also to hear from John Brittain; how they are doing and where they live. Old Mr. Ross and his wife was here about five weeks ago, left paper for me to write a letter to John. I told him I could not write soon, if ever, for my health has been poor this winter and I have had to be so much with the sick that I can hardly write for myself. I am very unwell today, and I expect Samantha will soon send for me, and be assured, I would write to none but you and my dear sister this day, but should you see John Ross, you can tell him his father is well. His stepmother I heard, was some out of health a day or so two ago.

I need to tell you a little about sister Hannah [Phillips Williams]. Poor girl, she has trouble. Her son-in-law was here three weeks ago, was going after a root doctor. His wife was thought to have the consumption and given up by the apothecary doctors. We have heard nothing from them since, but have not much hope ever hearing she is alive.

We have had a fairly cold winter for Ohio since first of December. It has been cold with the exception of a few moderate days. Good sleighing for near five weeks, but the snow has never been a foot deep. Grain and ... higher than ever was here before and likewise all other produce, still I think there will be enough for the cattle and folks. We have one yoke of oxen, three cows, two heifers, seventeen sheep, six lambs, and expect we shall have hay, oats and corn enough to bring them through and wheat for ourselves.

Henry's health has been good this winter, but poor Thomas is yet helpless and I think he is failing. Little Tommy is to his Aunt Betsy Carpenter's going to school. He was home four weeks ago. I expect he is well or we should of course, heard of it. I shall expect to have him home in sugaring, which we expect will be before a great while.

I have been looking for a letter from Tryphena Purdy [Hewitt Lee] or some of them, but get none. I can't think why they don't write. I have not heard a word from Mary Purdy Goodrich, since you wrote. Pray, write and let me know. My anxiety to hear from her, I can't describe. Give my love to Solomon Millard and Polly. Tell them I should be glad to see them and also James Tripp and his wife, but I have given up the idea of ever seeing them. I expect they are doomed to dig among the rocks and stones the rest of their lives.

I want to hear from Permelia Mullenix; where she lives and how they are doing and also from Lois Purdy and above all things, let me know if you ever hear from Francis Phillips, *[Ed. note: John Phillips grandson.]* for I have not heard from him in a long time and always forget to ask you about him when I write. Give my love to Polly Felts and family. How glad I would be to see them. My dear Nancy and Aurora [Clark], how oft I think of them. Remember my love to them, to Stephen Miller and family, to Comer and his. Silas Carey, I hardly know what to say about him, but should you see him, tell him I am the same and if he has forgot me, I never shall him. If I knew how to direct, I would write once more to him.

I return you my humble thanks for the precious lock of hair and don't forget a lock of my dear Lydia's. Thank you also for the papers. I should be very glad to get more, when convenient. As to religion, it is rather a low time at present, but I think there are yet some that enjoys this Heavenly portion. Henry has just returned from hearing a Baptist preacher. He is new coming. He preached in the Methodist schoolhouse. He liked him very much. We hope he will be the means of doing much good, but there is yet so much party spirit in almost all professor's breast, that I think it destroys much pure and undefiled religion, but dear brother, I am yet looking forward with great faith, believing that blessed time will come when the watchman shall see eye to eye, then the Christians shall all be of one heart and of one mind.

Dear brother and sister, I must now draw to a close by sending you my love and best wishes assuring you that my heart yet beats with all the affections of a sister and although we are separated, yet our hearts united by those sacred ties of both natural and Christian love that death shall never be able to destroy, and if we meet no more on earth, I fully believe we shall meet in Heaven, no more to take the parting hand. Farewell, believe me now and forever, your affectionate sister,

Henry and Mary Lott

I here with this send you a kiss.

P.S. I was at Joseph's [Lott] yesterday. Samantha [Lott] was not much [better]. I have not heard from her today. They all said give my love to your dear old brother and sister and try to [have] David Silsbee hear from us. Henry and I talk of going to Sunbury today. I shall leave a vacant spot and if I find a letter from Tryphena [Hewitt Lee] or any of them, I shall write and let you know. Henry sends his special spiritual to you and Lydia and says how glad he would be to see them. Thomas sends [love] and Abigail hers. Give my love to John Russell and Lavina, should you see them. Tell them not to be uneasy about Tommy, for he shall be taken care of.

May 15, 1837

My Dearest and Surely Best Beloved Brother and Sister,

Once more, I sit down to let you know we are alive and in common health, through the goodness of our Heavenly Father, though with sorrowful heart, I have to inform you that our dear sister Hannah [Phillips Williams] has been called to follow her daughter Lucena to the silent grave from whence no traveler ere returned. She had not seen eighteen years and had been married almost three years. *[Ed. note: I have been unable to determine her married name.]* She had a baby last September, but it died at six weeks old. She left no family but her husband. She was like the fair flower that fades before noon. The first cause of her sickness was the chill and fever; a year last winter they moved out to the Sandusky Plains. She was taken very sick two years ago, but got better so her father brought her home in one room before she was confined where she lived and died. She appeared much better the fore part of the winter but finely it terminated in that fatal disease, the consumption.

The first of April, Anson [Williams] came after me. The fifth day her happy spirit took its everlasting flight to those blest realms of eternal glory where pain and sorrow shall forever cease and none shall ever take the parting hand. The first of her sickness she seemed to think hard and say to those around her, "You can all live and I must die," but soon she seemed different and said, "Now, I am willing to die, for I believe Jesus has pardoned me and I shall go to Heaven and meet my dear babe."

I talked with her and gained full satisfaction the last she talked in connection, though she spoke sentences till almost the last breath. She called her father and mother and brothers and sisters to the bed and her other friends and took them by the hand, talked to them one by one, giving them some token of her affection and saying, "Farewell, remember dying Lucena, meet me in Heaven." And to her youngest sisters, she seemed to say the most. She reached her poor, white, dying hand and took hold of theirs and said, "Now, Elizabeth and Rebecca, remember the words of a dying sister. Be good children, obey your father and mother, be kind to one another and meet your sister in Heaven, where I am going," and truly her countenance bespoke Heaven. She seemed to drop asleep in the arms of Jesus.

Poor Hannah felt bad, but said, she had nothing to mourn for but her company. But she told [me] the night after she was buried as we sit up most of the night alone that I must write to you and give her best love to you and tell you that she never expected to see you in this world, but wished you not to forget her and pray for her, and that she believed she should meet you in glory and this hope which I think she has obtained is all the comfort she takes in this life.

I have been looking for them a long time, but they have none been here, nor I have heard nothing from them since John [Williams] brought me home the next day after the funeral. I must now tell you about Anny [Wheeler] and Samantha [Lott]. Anny has got about as well as she was before she was sick, but Samantha has been worse for some days past. I was there day before yesterday. She looks very miserable. We greatly fear she will never be well again. They send their love and best wishes to you and David Silsbee and would like to have you write and let them know the cause of his not living with the folks he had been living with for some lime.

Mr. Kimble's folks was all well last Sunday. Tommy [Russell] was there and he has gone again today. I have sent for Mrs. Kimble to come and help me pick wool. I expect she will be here tomorrow or next day. I seen Robert [Wells] and Harriett [Trumbull] the last of March and they were in common health, and send all the love and well wishes they can think of. Be assured this is not a little.

Brother Leonard [Lott] will start for Pennsylvania I expect in June on horseback or by water. He has not concluded which, but [you] may expect to see him, for he says he shall go and see you. I shall write by him, but don't fail of writing immediately on the receipt of this for we are very anxious to hear from you all and particular from my dear Mary and Tryphena Purdy [Hewitt Lee].

We have been looking for George Lee. If he should move to Illinois, tell him, he must come this way. I should like to know if Solomon Millard or James Tripp has sold or if they do ever talk of coming to this wonderful state of Ohio. We should like to know how the Spring has been with you, for I will assure you it has been the hardest here that ever was known. Frost and dry weather hung on till about ten days ago, when there came a rain that seemed to revive all nature. Today, we have had another. Peach trees are principally killed, but apple trees arc in full bloom and things look promising.

I must inform you that old Mrs. Hillman has left this world of sorrow and gone to the upper and better world. She died 26th of February. She had been blind several years. She went to go outdoors and fell off the steps, broke her arms and two or three of her ribs. Her fall, we think, was the cause of her death. It is a general time of health in this place. She that used to be Betsy Hutchings is well and sends her best respects and would like to hear from Jeremiah Blanchard's folks, for they have heard he was not expected to to live long with a fever sore. Likewise, would like to hear the certainty concerning her brother William, for since you wrote he was dead, she has heard he was alive.

I see old Mr. Ross and his wife not long since. They were well and if they live six months, they will have a young heir. You can act your pleasure about telling his children of it, but be assured it is true. He has bought a town about two miles from here, built and moved on it this spring. It is a new town called East Liberty. Mrs. Kimble gets no letters there. She, as well as ourselves, would like to hear from James Ross folks; where they are and how they are doing and also from her other friends. Finally, I want to hear from all. So write all you can.

I hope if I live till brother Leonard [Lott] returns, I shall hear more than either can write, but dear brother and sister, after all the satisfaction we do take in writing and seeing the eyes that has beheld each other, yet the pleasure of embracing each other, I fear will never be realized, but one thought yet gives sweet consolation of meeting in the fair climes of immortal glory where pain and sorrow shall never come, old age will never be felt, but we shall ever bloom in immortal youth, then we can count our sufferings over, no more to take the parting hand.

I wrote to you not long since that old Mr. John Budd and his wife was dead. I heard very correctly that he was alive and had got his thigh broke last week. He was near Sunbury when it was broke. He lives on Dunkins Plains about twelve miles from here. I should like to know how you made out with the suit in law concerning the farm you was like to lose when I was there. I am very glad to hear so good news from Francis [Phillips] and should be glad to hear from him again.

Thomas is yet helpless. He sends his love to you and often says how I want to see John and sister Lydia. Thomas Russell is well and grows like a weed. He appears contented and seldom speaks of his folks. I must now come to a close after sending our love and best wishes to you and dear sister Lydia and all your children. Forever, your affectionate brother and sister, farewell.

Henry and Mary Lott

This Book was Purchased, Jan. 4 — Anno Domini 1803. By John Phillips

June 4, 1837

Dear Brother and Sister,

The man that hands you these lines will be brother Leonard Lott. I need not say use him well, for I know you will and as I have wrote lately and he will tell you more than I can write, I shall write but a few lines to let you know, I am the same poor, old creature yet, but my heart still beats with all its former ardor for you. Still my affections are as great as ever. I feel bound to you and dear Lydia by more than earthly bounds for I feel bound by the tender ties of pure Christian love even that love which we have obtained by preservation which we received by mixture of the blood of our dear Redeemer that He spilt on Calvary and although we must be separated in body, yet we are bound by three fold chords that time, distance, not even the hand of death shall be able to dissolve for soon, I expect we shall be reunited in the father's Kingdom no more to take the parting hand.

If you have not wrote an answer to my last letter, do write by Leonard if you can, if he stays there long enough. If not, write when you can, particular about my dear Mary [Purdy], Tryphena [Hewitt Lee], and if any of them ever think of coming here, and if George Lee has returned, and what you have concluded about selling your property. If Leonard should go to Providence, don't forget to tell him to call to Silas Carey's for I hear nothing from him, but what you write and can't but think he would be glad to see him and hear from me, although he never writes, and I'm sure I should be glad to see one that has seen him.

Thomas Russell is well, sends his love to grandmother and grandfather, father and mother, brother and sisters. If Brother Leonard was going any way that it did not cost so much, he [Thomas] would go with him, but we can not get money enough by stage and water for times are pretty hard and money scarce since there is such work with the banks. I must now close after giving our love to all my friends and relatives. Believe me now and forever, your affectionate sister. Farewell, forget me not.

Henry and Mary Lott

November 26, 1837

My Dearest and Best Beloved Brother and Sister,

We received your very welcome and affectionate letter not long since and should have answered sooner, but the next Saturday Anson [Williams] and Hannah [Phillips Williams] and his oldest daughter that just moved from York State and her husband come here, stayed all night [Sarah and Isaac Bovee]. But Anson and his daughter and her husband went home next day, but left Hannah two weeks, the first visit I have ever had with her since they moved in and I fear it will be the last. Her health is very poor and more particular since her poor Lucena died. She said, "I feel Polly, as tho I was making you the last visit." We talked about you. She said she wanted to see you, but never expected to in this world but said I must give her love to you and hopes she will meet you in a better world than this. She seemed much altered and says she has a firm hope of meeting her dear Lucena where trouble and sorrow will never come.

Abraham Rosencranse took her home in a wagon and Henry and I went with her. Found all well and doing well as this world's goods and if Hannah ever gets to Heaven, and I do believe she will, it will surely be through much tribulations for certain it is that she lives in a house where much wickedness abounds. Grace shall much more abound or not, I can't say, but must leave it in the hands of Him that will judge both the quick and the dead, fully believing that He will reward every man according to [what] his work shall be.

Anna Wheeler went from here today. She returns you many thanks for writing about her brother, sends her love to you. Wants you should tell her brother to write to her, for she can't write herself and it is hard work to get anyone to write for her. Samantha [Lott] has had another very poor time, is some better now, but we have great reason to fear she will never be well again. I have not seen the Kimble's folks since got your letter, but heard they was well a week ago.

I started yesterday to old Mr. Ross, but could not get over the creek. The old gentleman has a very fine son two weeks old, its name- Nathan. I heard they was very smart and doing well. Thomas Russell is well and grows like a weed, sends his love to grandfather and grandmother, brothers and sisters, says he would like to see them, but don't want to go back again for he thinks it is cold enough here, tho we have had a very favorable fall thus far. We have had but two small snows yet.

I was in hopes of seeing some of my relatives when I read your letter, but have looked till I have given up all hopes. We was astonished when we heard the account of your crops, for be assured, it is not much like our Ohio crops. The corn and potatoes in particular. When we dug our potatoes, we had 73 bushels, all very good. We have the marlsets *[Ed. note: these are a type of potato.*], the apples [are] the moshanicks, the blues [corn] [have] ears more than 12 inches long and Abraham Rosencranse has larger yet, I dare not say how large for I don't know as you would believe me, but one thing I request of all that, except to come see for yourselves.

And now dear brother and sister, think me not crazy or out of my wits when I tell you, we have concluded that you had better sell your property in money and you can come nearly all the way by water. I have of late dreamed of seeing you both and it always appeared to be in Ohio and the thought will often come, who knows, but I shall see them here yet, but you have lived so long there, I well know it would be hard to make you think you could leave the place, but it seems as if it would be better if you could live the few days you have to stay in this unfriendly world where it was not winter all the year, but I fear my castles are all built in the air and like all the rest of my earthly pleasures, will fall to the ground. But, I leave all these things in the hands of Him that does things well, fully believing that when these earthly tabernacles shall fall, we have a house not made with hands, where I expect we shall meet, no more to part, forever.

My dear Mary [Purdy], I fear I shall never hear of her being alive again. How oft I think of her dear children, but I hope and pray they may look beyond earthly parents for consolation to Him that has promised to be the orphan's friend. Give my love to them when you see them. Tell them not to forget me. Also to Nancy and Aurora and Polly Felts and Silas Clark and Amanda [Miller] Parker; to Stephen Miller and wife and children. I would like to hear how Caleb Miller's widow and children do. I have not heard a word from them in a long time. Also from Amzi Wilson, whether he married again or not and where he lives. And Samuel Miller and Susannah and their children, should you ever see them; to Comer [Phillips] and family.

I can but hope you will see Silas Carey soon, but I think I shall write to him soon and jog his memory if I can possibly get a chance. Should you see John and Lavina Russell, give our love to them. We should be glad to see them for we are sure they could do better here than there.

Anson [Williams] said Cornwell [Phillips) yet lived in York State near where he has ever since he has been there. Said he was doing pretty well for a poor man in that country, but [says] Cornwell had the Ohio fever, but don't know whether he will ever be able to come or not. If he was here, he says he would let him have land to work as long as he lives and if Deborah and the children did not mow so great a swath, we should all be very glad to have them come and if it was not for that, I would write to him to find our brothers in Middlebury [Genesee Co. NY] for it is about ten miles to where *we* used to live. But I think if I live, I shall try to find time to write to them myself before I ... [*Ed. note: There is a Francis Phillips and a Zacharious Phillips on the 1820 New York census in Caldonia, Genesee County. It is possible that these are Mary's and John's brothers.*]

I should be glad if Dr. John Wilson's child could get well. Give my love to Lovisa and to Hosea [Phillips] when you see them, also to Sarah Wilson and her children. Let me know if Stephen Gautier and Merritt Wilson yet lives in Philadelphia and how are they? Your papers grow better and better for which I return you ten thousand thanks.

We are all in common health. Brother Thomas can walk some, but not able to do any work. He often talks about you; wishes he could see you. He says," Give my love to him. I never expect to see him, but I hope we shall both get to Heaven." I was up to Betsy Stark's today. They were all in common health. She sends her love to you. Would be glad to have a visit from you and Lydia. Should you see James Ross family, give our best respects to them; to John Brittain's should you see them.

Price of wheat from 75 cents to one dollar, corn from 25 cents to 31 cents per bushel, potatoes, 25 cents per bushel. I have not seen my dear Harriett [Trumbull] since last March, but Robert [Wells] was here not long since, said they were in common health. He read your letter; said don't forget to send my love to him. Brother Leonard Lott sends his best respects to you. Says he would like to see you in this goodly country where almost everything that is, grows.

I am very tired and it is getting late and Leonard is going to Sunbury early in the morning. I must draw to a close. Accept our love and best wishes for you and may you be cheered with the presence of the Lord and ever guided by His spirit the days you have to stay this veil of tears, and may you have a happy transport across the cold stream of Jordan into that celestial city where sorrow never comes. Your affectionate sister,

Mary and Henry Lott

P.S. Fail not of writing soon for we are very anxious to hear from you, but more particular from Mary.

CHAPTER VIII

I have tried to get time to finish this letter all week, but 10,000 cares has prevented me and I don't feel hardly able to sit up at this time...

March 5, 1838

My Dearest and Best Beloved Brother and Sister,

We have long been looking for a letter from you, but look in vain. We got the papers you sent, but no writing on them which we think you had sent a letter and we fear it has miscarried. We expect you will write immediately on the receipt of this and let us know how you all are, for we are very anxious to hear from in particular, Mary [Phillips Hewitt]. Oh dear, I fear we shall never hear she is alive, but why need I fear for you if her Heavenly Father has seen fit to call her home. Why should I murmur, for she has gone from a world of sorrow, pain and woe and joined her friends that has gone before to sing praises to God and the Lamb forever, no more to take the parting hand and in a few weeks or years at most, I expect to meet her where our Heavenly union shall be renewed, where there will be no sickness, no pain, no sorrow to interrupt our joy.

I read a letter from Mrs. Kimble's sister Elizabeth. She wrote that Soloman Millard, David Tripp and family had gone to Michigan, so I may give up all hopes of seeing any of my relatives in this country.

Samantha's health is some better, but we fear she will never be well, but she keeps up good courage and says she thinks she shall go to Pennsylvania yet and perhaps next summer, and says I must go with them to show them the way, but how that may be I can't say.

I have not seen Anny [Wheeler] since last fall. She is at Samantha's daughter's, Elsann. I heard she fell and almost broke her arm sometime ago, hurt her very bad, but is better. I have wanted to go and see her very much, but I am very much confined for I have no help but my two boys and they have been to school except when they had to help get wood, and be assured we have not burned a little for it has been the coldest weather for more than a month that has been since we have been here and the best sleighing, yet the snow has not been quite a foot deep. The fore part of the winter was warm and pleasant, but we have paid for it since. How long it will last, we can't say. It is cold and [there is] sleighing yet and looks very much like another snow storm.

We often talk about the folks in Pennsylvania and Thomas Russell often says it is cold enough here and I don't know what father's folks does if it is colder than here. Our health has been pretty good all winter. I have had some poor turns and Henry has had two, but neither to be confined.

Brother Thomas is much the same, not able to do anything and hard work to keep from freezing as he thinks by the fire. We have not heard from Anson's folks since 8th, January. [When] Anson was here, they were in common health. Then we have looked for them ever since sleighing, but they don't come. Henry will go out there in a few days, but no way for poor me to go. He was down to my dear Harriett's not long since. She has been very unwell a long time, but it will be a year the 28th day of this month since I have seen her. No way contrived for to go and none to do while I am gone.

Thomas Russell is 14 years this month. We don't know what day. We wish you could find out and let us know. We have heard a report that there was something for the heirs, the poor sufferers on the Susquehanna. I expect you know all about our father suffering as well as your own and likewise, if there is a chance to get anything, please let us know in your next, for if there is anything we can get lawfully, poor Cornwell and I needs it perhaps more than the rest, but should anything be got, I think each one has an equal right and I am willing all should share alike.

[Ed. note: In 1792 half a million acres was given to citizens of the Connecticut Reserve who lost land to the British during the Revolutionary War at New London, New Haven and elsewhere. The lands and people were referred to as "sufferers." The people in Pennsylvania had also petitioned the government for lands lost by those who were members of the Susquehanna or Connecticut Land Company. Francis Phillips, the father of Mary and John, was a member of that group.]

Let me know if you have heard anything from Stephen Gautier or Merritt Wilson lately, Lois Purdy, and also if you have heard from Solomon Millard and David Tripp since they went away. If they would write and let me know how to direct, I should be very happy to keep up a correspondence with them.

The Presbyterians have had a protracted meeting and it lasted almost two weeks, nite and day. There was near forty moved forward and about twenty professed to obtain a hope in Jesus. May they ever stand fast in that liberty where with Christ has made them free. [*Ed. note: Historians have noted that the Presbyterian religion was "...among the best organized in pioneer Ohio." The Methodists were circuit riders who used camp meetings as their means of ministering. Mary refers to meetings in her letters. Her family were apparently Baptists whose preachings were very successful on the frontier.*]

We return you many thanks for your papers. We think them very good and their opinion on slavery exactly with my mind, for ever since I come to years of understanding, I believe slavery a great evil and an abomination in the eyes of our Heavenly Father, and for such enmity to be suffered in a nation that has been so cried up for a land of liberty. And I do believe if something is not done soon to alleviate the sufferings of the poor slaves, that the Lord will deliver them as he did the children of Israel some way or another, and as a nation we shall be scourged, for the beautiful true liberty [will] no more flourish, for the limbs are already loped and the leaves are withering.

Dear brother, I dreamed of seeing you the other night. I told you that I feared I should make a ... a dream as I often had before. You told me no, and took me in your arms and kissed me and said, "it is me," but when I woke, I found it a dream. But if my dream can never be realized on earth, I fully believe it will be in Heaven, where we shall no more take the parting hand. Give our love to each child, grandchild and great-grandchild and accept the same yourselves and believe as now and forever, your affectionate brother and sister.

Henry and Mary Lott

I shall write again soon.

January 1840

My Dear and Best Beloved Brother and Sister,

We received your very welcome letter not long since. It rejoiced our hearts to hear you was alive and as well as can be expected for people of your age. May the Lord spare your lives, May He keep you as under the shadow of his wing and oh, that it might be His will for us to meet once more in this veil of tears. How I would press you both to this fond bosom, but money is so scarce that I fear that can never be, but I wish to say not my will, but His be done and wait with resignation, looking forward to that glad day when I trust we shall meet in the blissful climes where parting will be no more.

I will now tell you we are all in common health. Anna Wheeler is also well for one of her age. She lives with us this winter and how much longer I can't say. She come here in the fall and wanted to stay, and Henry told her she might have half she would spin as we had a pretty good crop of flax, and I shall weave it if I am well. She does chores to pay me for weaving. She has got 27 yards spun and would have had more, but the boys go to school and Henry can't keep her in flax and what else he has to do, and brother Thomas is almost helpless and very near blind in his other eye.

Anne sends her thanks and love to you and her brother David. Tell him [he] must come and see you when he wants to hear from her, as there appears to be no way of correspondence between them. I am glad John [Russell] got a little of his father's property, tho a small share to what he ought to had.

I have not seen old Mr. Ross since I got your last letter. Heard they was all well and as to the judgement you wrote about, he never can pay for. He is very poor and has hard work to live. If you can get it of his son [John Ross], you had better. If you can't, you will have to lose it for all getting it of him You wrote that Mr. Ross was very sick. We should like to know which of his sons it was and how he is.

The Kimble's folks are all well now, but Mr. Kimble has been sick all the fall and part of the winter, and their boy has been very sick a long time, was not that he would live. It has been some sickly, but few died. Two children is all that has died near, but a solomn service took place in Sunbury a week ago last night. James Greglery, a very wealthy smart young man of a very respectful family cut his own throat; lived out three hours. He had appeared to be deranged by turns for some time. Brother Leonard and family are all in common health. He sends his respects to you. Samantha's health is better than it has been in three years.

Henry has had the thrashing machine and thrashed his oats out in a day, about one hundred bushel, but they won't bring money at any price. I wish we had them there, but our ... like all other castles built in air, falls to the ground and we shall get nothing for them, nor of old Mr. Ross to help us there, but it may be possible times will take a turn and we shall yet see you this side of the grave. It would be the greatest satisfaction I could enjoy in this life to go and see you and your children and grand and great-grand children.

How often I think of Nancy and Aurora [Clark]. So give my love to them. Kiss their babes for me; to Polly Felts and her girl that lives with you, and Preserved Taylor, and to John and Lavina Russell; to Lois [Miller] and her husband. Let me know how many there is of the five generations. Give my love and best wishes to Mr. Goodrich. Tell him I often think of him and would like to know who lives with him, and if DeWitt [Phillips] is married and where Louis [Miller] lives, and also where Isaac [Hewitt] lives; if Comer [Phillips] has moved. My love to Susannah [Miller) and Stephen Miller and his wife and children and finally, all that inquires for me.

I have heard that Sabra Bates was dead, would like to the truth. I wonder if you know Peter and Nathaniel Richards that lives in the Green woods near James Ross? If you ever see them, tell them their brother Cornelius lives our nearest neighbor. They are all well and [a] very fine family they are. They have built a very elegant white house last summer and moved in last fall.

Now dear brother, I must draw to a close. After our love and good wishes, we subscribe ourselves your most affectionate, tho unworthy brother and sister.

Henry and Mary Lott

P.S. Now dear brother, don't fail of writing, for I hardly know how to wait. It is near eleven o'clock and nite. I am very tired. My eyes fail me, farewell. Do you think the heirs of the sufferers will ever get anything? I wish they might and perhaps I might come and see you.

If you see David Silsbee, before you write, ask him what year his mother died in? Anna Wheeler forgot and she wants to know. I have not seen any of Anson's folks since I wrote last, but heard not long since, they was all well except Hannah's oldest daughter had a child, very sick.

We have not heard from Cornwell [Phillips] in a long time. Mrs. Kimble got a letter from her sister yesterday and Mr. Kimble brought it here today for me to see. She wrote you as well. We have had but little snow, but some pretty cold days and nites. I can't tell you the price of grain in … for it won't fetch money at any price. I wish the Van Burens will get tired of their fun in stopping the banks for some of them will begin to want money as well as others. [*Ed. note: Banking problems continued throughout the state until at least 1840. The U.S. Bank ceased to function in March of 1836. In 1837, a panic followed, and Ohio banks suspended specie payments. Barter again became the means of existence.*]

Purdy 5	Erastus 1	[torn] 3
Minerva Fish 4	Caleb 4	
Martha 2	Dorcas 1	
Eliphas 2	Nancy 4	
Sanford 3	Aurora 3	
William 2	John T 2	

[*Ed. note: This list probably refers to John's Great-grandchildren.*]

KINGSTON OLD BLUE PRESBYTERIAN CHURCH, 1827, DELAWARE COUNTY, OHIO

March 29, 1840

My Ever Dear Brother and Sister,

We received your very welcome letter and was very glad to hear you was yet alive and as well as you are, but Permelia's [Tripp] children, I often think of them. I would like to know how many she had and where they are. I should have answered your letter sooner, but when we got it, brother Leonard [Lott] lay very sick, but he is now better. He sends his best respects to you.

I have been perusing the papers all over and over and am sorry to say, I can't find your receipt, but hope you will find it yet, [because] I can't bear to think you should have it to pay again. I have begun to look for Brother Cornwell, [Phillips] but don't see him and fear it will be too good luck for me to ever see him here as I am always looking for disappointment so long as I stay on these lone grounds where sorrows grow. I will now tell you that through the goodness of our Heavenly Father, we are in common health, except brother Thomas. He has taken a heavy cold and is very unwell. It has fell in his other eye and it is almost blind.

There has been a protracted meeting a week and members went forward to be prayed for and among them, Tommy [Russell] went. He appears very sober and very different from what he ever was before. Help me to pray that he may be truly converted and be a follower of our dear Redeemer. He is now gone to a funeral, one about his own age.

Dear brother, I begun this letter last Sunday. I told you brother Thomas was very unwell, is now very sick and no prospect of his ever being better in this world. I have tried to get time to finish this letter all week, but 10,000 cares has prevented me and I don't feel hardly able to sit up at this time, but I must try to close it today and send it to Post Office in the morning, for I know you are waiting with anxiety, but you must pardon my seeming neglect.

Anny Wheeler lives here yet, is well and sends her love and thanks to you. She wants you should ask her brother David [Silsbee], what year, what month, and what day of the month, her mother died for she has forgot and would thank you if you would write and let her know.

We have had but very little snow this winter, some pretty cold weather, some very heavy thunderstorms for a week or two past, one last nite. We have made about 120 weight and some molasses. Money is scarce as ever and sugar will be about as scarce.

Samantha Lott has got smarter than she has been in three years, sends her best respects to you. We should be glad to hear from James and Siley [Silence] Brown, if you could afford to write. I have not seen the Kimble's folks since I received your last letter. They have fifty acres of land in Bennington [Ohio] about five miles from here and moved on it 1st of February. Old Mrs. Ross was here since I got your last letter. I told her what you had wrote. She said they would be willing to pay it if they could, but they have nothing and had hard work to live. The old gentleman Ross is willing to work, but is old and not able. He is now very unwell. Betsy Stark sends her love to you and sister Lydia. Says she hopes you will not forget her. Give my love to Trypheny [Hewitt Lee] and her husband when you see them, to Nancy and Aurora [Clark] to John and Polly and little Catherine that lives with you. Tell her she must be a good girl and do everything grandfather and grandmother wants her to and the Lord will love her, as well as everybody else.

If you see Susannah Miller, give my love to her. Tell her I have looked for an answer to the letter I sent her last fall, but begin to think I never shall get it. My love to Stephen Miller and children. I would like to know how Amanda [Miller Parker] comes on. I would write to John and Lavina Russell, but it seems almost impossible to get a chance, but give my love and best wishes to them. We should be glad if they would write to us. I should like to know if his half sister Rethena [Russell] is living and where she is and if his stepmother is alive and how they received him when he went there. Thomas is groaning. I must draw to a close.

Our love and best wishes to you and sister Lydia and to all my friends and the friends of Zion. I must say I am now and forever, your affectionate sister till I meet you on that happy shore where sin and pain is felt no more, no more to grieve, no more to part, where death nor sickness ever come, but we shall in that safe home rest.

Henry and Mary Lott

P.S. Fail not of writing immediately on the receipt of this. No Cornwell yet. If he is there when this arrives, tell him he must hurry on or I fear he will never see Thomas and he wants to see him very much.

1842 or early 1843; Letter is not all there, and the date is missing.

[Ed. note: There are letters missing between this one and the last in 1840. Lydia Tripp Harding Phillips died sometime during that year. John Phillips married Bathsheba Green on October 27, 1842 when he was 90 years of age, This letter is addressed to John and Bathsheba, so it was written after that date.]

...they said they should be here in current time, they are and we have plenty of them. Dear brother, more than one week has passed away since I began this letter. I have had a very sick turn, but got better in a day or two, but there has been and still is distressing time at one of our near neighbors, Mr. Anways. Tommy [Russell] will know who they are. The old man and woman and three children are all down with the measles and their son-in-law [Mr. Dyer] moved in to take care of them. And part of them are down and none of them has never had them. I have been there twice a day, every day for more then a week. I have been there this forenoon and must go again toward nite, but I was determined to finish my letter, unless they send for me.

The drought continues yet very hard. Very dull prospects for corn or anything else... Banks will soon have done sailing over this rough tho short journey of life and safely land on the other side of the cold stream of Jordan in that fair land of eternal repose, no more to part.

Give my love to Tommy Russell, his father, mother, brother and sisters. Tell them, 1 [am] yet the same. To Susannah Miller, Stephen and family; I hope she is better. To Nancy and Aurora [Clark], James Tripp and family, Comer [Phillips] and family and finally to all those you see that inquires after me, but particular to Elder Miller. Henry, Thomas, Robert [Wells] and Isaac [Dayton Tanner] all join with me in love to you and sister and they say particular to Tommy. I must close, my head aches. I must go to visit the sick. We remain your affectionate brother and sister. *[Ed. note: It is apparent that Thomas Russell returned to his home in Pennsylvania sometime between the date of the last letter and this.]*

Henry and Mary Lott

September 10, 1843

My Dear Brother and Sister,

Once more, I sit down to let you know we are yet alive. Henry's health is yet poor, tho keeps about and works some. My health is some better than when I last wrote, but have many poor turns. Brother Thomas is yet as helpless and as much trouble as ever. Isaac [Dayton Tanner] is pretty well at present. Robert Wells is with us yet. His eyes some better, so he has been a weaving for me, which helps me much for I have no girl to help me and have my housework and spinning to do myself.

We received your welcome letter a short time since, was very glad to hear you was alive, but sorry to hear you was both so feeble and you so lame, but hope you are better. Expecting to hear the thing that will surprise us. We have all guessed and perhaps none guessed right. Isaac guessed you would come here or Tommy Russell would be married, but his being married would not surprise us, but your coming would almost overcome us, but that I can't expect. Robert guessed you would have an heir, but I told him sister's age [57 years] [and] then he said, it might be a miracle like Sarah of old, but for my part, I believe I will not tell what I guessed at present, but wait till I get the next letter, for I hope you will live to write a good many, yet I must now tell you I have been to see Ann Wheeler and read your letter and I was very glad to hear from her brother David Silsbee, and particular from her uncle that she had not heard from in so long.

Her health is pretty good at present. She and her daughter and her husband send their love to you and return you many thanks for your favors in writing to them and wishing to be remembered to David Silsbee should you see him, and we expect he will come when he hears you get the letter.

You wrote it was hard getting money there. It is the same or worse here. We can sell nothing for money, and we owing and have enough to sell if we could get the money at any resonable price, we might pay our debts and help ourselves to some things we need, but so it is and how long times will remain so, I can't say, but I expect if I live, I shall see harder before we see better and so I try to get along the best way we can. *[Ed. note: Ohio created a State Bank in 1845. Until then, hard times continued.]*

We have had a great drought here. It was thought one spell, there would be little or no corn, but of late, there has been showers pretty often and there is like to be a good many good crops. We have had very warm weather for a long time till last nite and today it is almost cold enough for great coats.

l have not heard from Anson's folks in a long time. I have looked for them here all summer, look in vain. Isaac [Tanner] has gone to Mr. Trumbull's and if none of Anson's folks come here in a week or two, I shall send him to see if they are alive. So I can hear from them, for it seems as tho I can never go to see them, athough I have no other sister nor brother that I can go to see, and I hear nothing from Cornwell [Phillips], but dear brother and sister, if you was as near me as they are, my anxiety to see you is so great, if there was no other way to get to you before tomorrow nite, I should be there ... but alas 500 miles, hills and rivers and vales separates our poor bodies but distance, time, nor even the monster king of terror can not separate the tender tie of affection to which our souls are bound.

Oh Lord, reconcile me to all things and help me to look beyond this veil of tears where we shall meet no more to part. Give my love to Tommy [Russell] , his father, mother, sisters and Albert [Russell]. To Susannah, Stephen Miller and family, Nancy and Aurora [Clark]. I'm sorry A ... health is so poor. Comer, Hosea and all the rest that ever inquire for us. I heard from Mrs. Kimble not long since, her health is some better, but not good. We haven't heard from old Mr. Ross since he moved to his son Samuel's.

I must draw to a close. Accept our love and best wishes and believe us now and forever your affectionate brother and sister,

Henry and Mary Lott

P.S. I would like to know if Sarah Wilson has ever been to see you yet and if she lives with her sons and on your farm in Carbondale, or if they have farms of their own. Please let me know if you hear from Silas Carey's mother. Also let us know if Tommy lives at home this summer.

[Ed. note: There are letters missing between this one and the next, March, 1846. Henry Lott died May 1844.]

CHAPTER IX

I can't write much more, but will if I live, answer all that comes from there.

March 27, 1846

My Ever Dear Brother and Sister,

I have sit down to let you know that I am yet alive, while many of our friends are gone, no more to return and dear brother, I had long given up all hopes of ever hearing that you was alive or even hearing from any of my friends in them parts, for it is near a year since I received your last letter. I have wrote four or five requesting some of the relatives to write if you was dead or if you could not [write]. I went or sent to the Post Office every week for I can't say how long, but no letter, at length, gave up all hopes and got one wrote to send to that Post Master thinking he would write and let hear from you at least, but just as I was going to send it, to my joy and surprise, in come a letter from Lavina and Tommy and Polly Parker and with it come the joyful tidings that you was alive and well.

Oh, brother, could I but see you once more and clasp you to this fond heart and bosom, all the sorrows and afflictions I have called to pass thru since last I saw you, I could for a moment forget my pain, but I don't know as that can ever be. I must live alone in one sense, no relative other than Hannah and her children. No, my dear brother Thomas is gone to the land from whence no traveler ere returned, the 17th of February at 4 o'clock in the afternoon without a groan or struggle. His happy soul took its flight to the happy regions where sickness and pain and sorrow never come. I was the only relative to follow him to the silent tomb. He was carried to the Methodist meeting house, sermon preached by Elder Wigton; a Baptist buried in the Methodist graveyard by the side of my bosom friend, leaving room between them for me should I die near here.

Dear brother and sister, will you think of poor me, how lonesome I am? My once family, all consumed to the silent grave. I am very anxious to see you all once more and had I the wherewithal, I would try one more journey to see you this summer. If I could light of good company, and don't know but I might try it alone, although I am too old. But why do I dwell on fancy or castles in the air that may never prove a reality?

I wish you would have some of your children or grandchildren when they write, come to your house as Lavina says you can't see to write yourself. Perhaps she or Tommy will be the one. Tell them to write what town and county Deathic Hewitt lives in for I think I shall go with Mr. Trumble's folks when they move to Michigan this winter or next spring and if I like, perhaps I shall move there and I shall try to find him out. I want to know if James Tripp lives there; if so, give my love to them; to Stephen Miller and family; to Susannah, to Comer and family; to Aurora and hers; to Amanda and all that asks after me.

I should like to hear from James Ross and family. His father's family was well not long ago since and Mr. Kimble's. Anna Wheeler is in common health. She wants to hear from her brother. Joseph Lott and his wife's health is very good. She is doctoring for cancer on her breast.

I went to Anson's soon after Thomas died. John Williams has been very sick, seven months. I fear he will never get well. I have not heard from them since I was there. I am looking for some of them soon. Hannah's health is very poor and she is almost blind. Anson has been sick with chill and fever, is better, but has rheumatism bad. He is not able to labor, but hobbles about some. The rest was in common health.

The winter has been very hard. There has been the deepest snow that was ever known in this part of Ohio. It has been about a foot deep and perhaps more. We would like to know how deep it has been there. It is a very poor sugar spring. We have made but little and expect to make but little and perhaps no more.

I can't write much more, but will if I live, answer all that comes from there. My love to Deborah [Doud Phillips] and children. Tell her to write and I will answer it. Dear brother, try to write a line in their letter. I can read it, be it ever so poor, and one line from your dear hand will do me so much good. Accept my love and best wishes and believe me now and forever, your most affectionate sister.

Mary Lott

Deacon John Phillips Obituary

Wilkes-Barre Advocate - **September 16, 1846**

DIED

In Abington, on Friday, the 4th of September last, 1846, Deacon John Phillips at the age of ninety-four years and eight months. His remains were interred on Sabbath following, in the burying ground at the Baptist Church in Abington, attended by a large assemblage of relatives and friends. Divine service was performed by Rev. John Miller.

We cannot know if Mary received word of John's death and the tragedy of the news was too much for her to bear, or if her body could just no longer handle the struggle of life alone without help other than Isaac Tanner, the bound boy she apparently raised as her own.

It is certain that Mary suffered from an ailment, perhaps a heart condition. It is apparent from her letters that she expressed her constant fear of John's death.

It is my own belief that Mary did indeed receive the news from family members of John's passing, and the sorrow, especially after the recent loss of her brother Thomas, brought on her own death.

Mary passed away sometime before September 30, 1846, to be "reunited in that fair haven of eternal repose, where sorrow never comes and parting sounds was never heard."

DATES OF DEATH

Zephaniah Lott died 26 February 1829

Else Lott died 7 December 1836

Lydia Tripp Harding Phillips died 1840

Henry Lott died 13 May 1844

Cornwell Phillips died by 1846

Thomas Simmons Phillips died 17 February 1846

Deacon John Phillips died 4 September 1846

Mary Phillips Lott died by 30 September 1846

Anson Williams died 28 March 1847

Hannah Phillips Williams died 12 August 1851

Rebecca Williams Faulknor died 17 February 1857

APPENDIX

THE FAMILY OF ZEPHANIAH LOTT

ZEPHANIAH LOTT b. 14 March 1742, Northampton, Bucks, Pennsylvania; d. 26 February 1829, Kingston, Delaware, Ohio. Buried in Stark Cemetery, Porter Township, Delaware, Ohio. (b & d dales tombstone inscriptions) Son of Henry and Mercy Lott. (IGI) Married

ELSE VAN PELT (1) b. 11 September 1750, (prob. Bucks Co. PA); d. 4 December 1836 (b & d dates tombstone inscription) Kingston, Delaware, Ohio. Buried in Stark Cemetery, Porter Township, Delaware, Ohio.

CHILDREN (2)

Henry (Henderick) (m) b. 1773; C. 24 April 1774, Reformed Nether(lands) Dutch Church, Southampton, Bucks, Pennsylvania. (IGI)

d. 13 May 1844, Kingston, Delaware, Ohio. Buried in Stark Cemetery, Porter Township, Delaware, Ohio. m. Mary [Phillips] b. 2 August 1780-90; (on 1830 census, between 50-60; on 1840 census, between 50-60; birthdate-per letter); d. by 30 September, 1846. (will) Location of grave unknown.

Zephaniah (Sephenia) (m) C. 10 March,1776; Reformed Netherlands) Dutch Church, Southampton, Bucks, Pennsylvania. (IGI)

John (m) b. 1777; d. 3 July 1849, Kingston, Delaware, Ohio. Buried in Stark

Cemetery, Porter Township, Delaware, Ohio. (1*)

Leonard (3) (m) b. 1779; d. September 1842, Kingston, Delaware, Ohio Buried in Stark Cemetery, Porter Township, Delaware, Ohio (per letter; brother Leonard) m. Elizabeth, b.1785; d. 4 May 1847, Kingston, Delaware, Ohio. Buried in Stark Cemetery, Porter Township, Delaware, Ohio.

Caty (4) C 21 April 1781; Nether(lands) Dutch Church, Southampton, Bucks, Pennsylvania. (IGI)

Stephen (m) C. 14 Nov 1784; Reformed Nether(lands) Dutch Church, Southampton, Bucks, Pennsylvania. (IGI) (5)

Joseph (m) C. 1 July 1787; Nether(lands) Dutch Church, Southampton, Bucks, Pennsylvania. (IGI) d. 1 March 1881, Kingston, Delaware, Ohio. Buried in Stark Cemetery, Porter Township, Delaware, Ohio. m. Samantha, b. 1788; d. 31 August 1851, Kingston, Delaware, Ohio. Buried in Stark Cemetery, Porter Township, Delaware, Ohio. (6)

Sarah (Sally) (f) C. 1790; d. 3 May 1854. buried Old Blue Cemetery, Kingston Township, Delaware, Ohio m. Thomas Camey (son of John & Mary E. Carney) b. 1795; d. 1860. (on 1840 Kingston, Del, 0 census (7)

Isaac (m) b. & d. unknown. M Eliza Residence on 1820 Census, Windham Twp., Luzerne Co., PA. (8)

TOMBSTONE INSCRIPTIONS - Delaware County, Ohio

STARK CEMETERY - PORTER TOWNSHIP

Lott, Joseph, d. Mar. 1, 1881, aged 94 yrs
Samantha, his wife, d. Aug. 31, 1851, ae 63y 7m 4d
Lott, Henry, d May 13, 1844 ae 70y 6m 5d
Lott, Leonard, d. Sept /, 1842 aged 62y 1 lm 12d
his wife Elizabeth, d. May 4, 1847, aged 62y 3 m
Carney, James, d. Nov. 25, 1841?, aged 22y 4 m--da
Lott, Else, wife of Zephaniah, b. Sept. 11, 1750, d. Dec. 4, 1836
Zephaniah, b. Mar. 14, 1742, d. Feb. 26, 1829
Lott, John, d. July 3, 1849, aged 71y 8m 17d
Stark, James, d. June 30, 1859, ae 79y 11m 28d
Elizabeth, wife of J., d. Aug. 19, 1852 ae 68y
Cornelia E., dau of J. & E.W., d. Apr. 12, 1839 ae 13 y 7m

ELSE VAN PELT LOTT

A deposition for a Revolutionary War Pension claimed by the surviving Lott family members was given 19 May, 1848. Stephen R Bennett of Delaware, Ohio told that he and his partner James L. Gregory, deceased made the grave clothes for Else Lott and the date of her death is recorded in his book. In a deposition given 19 May, 1848 Rev. Ahab Jinks of Delaware, Ohio said that he preached the funeral sermon for Else Lott. In a deposition given 19 May, 1848, Benjamin Newberry of Delaware, Ohio says that he "undertook" and got widow Else Lott's grave clothes. In a deposition given 20 May, 1848, Moses Decker of Delaware, Ohio told that he made the coffin for Else Lott and the date of her death is recorded in his book. Isaac Finch, Thomas Jenkins, and Solomon Whitcomb also appear in affidavits for the same period testifying to being acquainted with the widow and her husband. (9)

REFERENCES

(1) Per Cemetery book-stones were knocked over (Tl-Del. Co.) DAR record – Zephaniah Lott Rev. War soldier-Bucks PA Militia. Roster 1, p.231 and Roster III, p.222. 58th NSDAR Report. Names of children per DAR Roster.

(2) See Rev. War Pension R 6458; document dated May 3, 1848 which refers to widow Else Lott, deceased and" following named children now survive her, being her only children now surviving," Zephaniah Lott of ..., Seneca Co., NY, Stephen Lott, Tunkhannock Twp., Wyoming Co. PA, Isaac Lott of Forkston Twp., Wyoming Co., PA, Joseph Lott, John Loll and Sarah Carney of Kingston, Delaware Co., 0. Henry and Leonard deceased; no further information on Caty.

(3) Names in italics have not had relationship proven, although Leonard is mentioned in letters as" brother Leonard." There is also a Leonard Lott on the 1830 census in Windham, Luzerne, PA showing M; 2- 20 to 30, 1 - 50 to 60; F; 1 - 10 to 15. Henry's relationship is established in letters and NSDAR Official Roster III, p. 222.; 58th NSDAR Report.

(4) No further record found.

(5) Relationship proven per an application for pension dated May 3, 1848 for his father Zephaniah Lott's service in Revolutionary War. Stephen was residing in Wyoming Co., PA.

(6) Per War of 1812 pension, Survivor Certificate 24305, Joseph enlisted in Luzerne Co., PA and served as a Lieutenant in Captain J. Camp's Company of Pennsylvania Militia from November 3, 1814 to November 24, 1814. He received a pension on his application dated May 14, 1878 while a resident of Kingston, Delaware Co., O. Will of 27 February, 1849 names nephew Daniel S. Carney, Brother Joseph Lott, sister Sarah Camey. Executors Joseph Lott and Daniel Carney.

(7) Sarah's age on grave marker shown as "'aged 64 y, 3 m, 24 d.'"' Mary E. Carney's grave marker says"' wife of John Carney of Pan.,d. June 9, 1852, aged 93y." She was mother of James and Thomas Camey, husband of Sarah Lott. [Pan may mean Pennsylvania] There is also a marker for Thomas Camey, d. 15 April, 1862, aged 26y, 9m, 28d. Possibly a son of Thomas and Sarah. James Carney d. 28 September, 1828, aged 31y, 1m, 11d. His wife was Jane Ostrander, b. 1800, d.1880, who married 2nd Richard Waldron. James and Jane Carney had four sons; Theodore, Thomas, who became Gov. of Kansas during Civil War. His name was also spelled Kearney, (TI-Del. Co.) LeRoy, and Creighton. There is also a marker in Stark Cemetery, Porter Township, Delaware, Ohio in the Lott burial plot for James Carney, d. 25 November, 1841(?) (illegible) aged 22y, 4m, --- d. Possibly a son of Thomas.

(8) Relationship proven by Power of attorney "to our trusty and loving son Isaac Lott," Deed Book 19, p. 677, Wyoming Co., PA. Dated 21, October, 1817. Recorded 17 April, 1820. Signed by Zephaniah and Else Lott. Witnessed by Joseph Lott and David Perkins, Luzerne Co. Power of attorney for Isaac Lott dated 1 January, 1853, Twp of Forkston, Wyoming Co. PA, names Eliza Lott as claimant, perhaps his wife.

(9) This information is found in the request for Revolutionary War Pension #R6458

THE FAMILY OF FRANCIS PHILLIPS

FRANCIS PHILLIPS b. 29 July, 1720; W. Greenwich, Kent, RI; d. after 1788, (1) probably PA.
Married 22 January, 1745.
1st, DEMIS AYLESWORTH (2) b. 22 January, 1725; E. Greenwich, (CO.?) RI, daughter of Arthur and Mary Franklin Aylesworth, (Austin); d. Probably by 1761. (3) Other wive's names unknown. (4)

CHILDREN
- I. John (m) b. 4 January, 1752, (new calendar) 24 December, 1751 (old calendar) Beekman Twp., Dutchess, NY; (pension). d. 4 September, 1846, Abington, Luzerne, PA. Buried Hickory Grove Cemetery, Abington, Luzerne, PA. m. 1st, Mary Chamberlain(check spelling) 20 January, 1771, b. 27 July, 1745; (IGI) (Bible?), d. 9 November, 1815, Abington, Luzerne, PA (check date) Buried Hickory Grove Cemetery, Abington, Luzerne, PA. m. 2nd, Lydia Tripp Harding 17 November, 1816, Abington, Luzerne, PA.; b.1770 or 6 September, 1762, Warwick, Providence, RI, d. 1840. Buried Hickory Grove Cemetery, Abington, Luzerne, PA. m. 3rd, Bathshebah Green, 27 October, 1842, Abington, Luzerne, PA. b. c. 1775; d. after 1846.

It is believed that these are children by a second wife.
- II. Francis b. c. 1760 - 65, New York State; d. after 24 April, 1832, prob. Washington Co. New York; m. Mary• ·. b. prob. New York State; d. after 24 April, 1832, prob. Washington Co. New York. (5)
- III. Zacheous
- IV. Thomas
- V. Mary b. c. 1782; d. by 30 September, 1846. (will) m. Henry Lott, date unknown, son of Zephaniah Lott and Else Van Pelt, b. 1773; C. 24 April, 1774, Reformed Nether(lands) Dutch Church, Southampton, Bucks, Pennsylvania. d. 13 May, 1844, Kingston, Delaware, Ohio. Buried in Stark Cemetery, Porter Township, Delaware, Ohio.
- VI. Cornwell b. c. 1786-90 d. between 1843-1846. m. Deborah Doud, daughter of Isaac and Elizabeth Osborne Doud), date unknown. (1830 Genesee Co. New York census shows 8 children; 5 m ten and under; 3 f ten and under.) Known children are Isaac, William, Hannah, Elizabeth.

JOHN PHILLIPS (m) b. 4 January, 1752 (new calendar), 24 December, 1751 (old calendar) Beekman Twp., Dutchess, NY (pension). d. 4 September, 1846, Abington, Luzerne, PA. Buried Hickory Grove Cemetery, Abington, Luzerne, PA. m. 1st, MARY CHAMBERLAIN, 20 January, 1771; b. 27 July, 1745; ([GI) (Bible), d. 9 November, 1815, Abington, Luzerne, PA. Buried Hickory Grove Cemetery, Abington, Luzerne, PA.

CHILDREN

1. Martha (f) b. 21 October, 1771; Pownal, Bennington, VT. d. unknown, m. 16 December, 1789 John Tripp.
2. Susanna (f) b. 7 August, 1773; Pownal, Bennington, VT. d. 10 August, 1849. Buried Marcey Cemetery, Hughestown, (Luzerne), PA. m. 7 September, 1788, Samuel Miller b. 1767; (NSDAR) Dutchess Co. NY, d. 9 April, 1839. Buried Marcey Cemetery, Hughestown, (Luzerne) PA.
3. Sarah (Salla) (f) b. 29 July, 1775, Pownal, Bennington, VT.; d. 1855. m. 7 February, 1793/ 4, Isaac Wilson b. 2 August, 1768; (NSDAR), Basking Ridge, NJ, d. 1845.
4. Mary (Molly) (f) b. 4 May, 1778; PA d. before 1841.m. 1st, 18 February, 1794, Isaac Hewitt d. c. 1808. m. 2nd, Ephriam Purdy, m. 3rd, Seth Goodrich, b. Wayne, PA
5. Hosea (m) b. 28 May, 1781, Wilkes-Barre, PA; d. 25 October, 1858 Justus (Lackawanna) PA. m. 1st, 28 October, 1799, Lavinna Davis, m. 2nd, 21 November, 1851

(WHGS) Mrs. Elizabeth Smith Fish, daughter of Benjamin and Abigail Smith b. c. 1787; d. 8 April, 1856.

6. Comer (m) b. 24 December, 1783; d.19 January, 1847. m.5 February 1807, Hannah Mott, daughler of -- Mott, b. 2 January, 1779; (NSDAR), d. 27 March, 1853, Taylor, PA. (NSDAR)

m. 2nd, 17 November, 1816, Abington, Luzerne, PA. LYDIA TRIPP HARDING, b.1770 or 6 September, 1762, Warwick, Providence, RI; d. 4 December, 1840. Buried Hickory Grove Cemetery, Abington, Luzerne, PA.

m. 3rd, 27 October, 1842, Abington, Luzerne, PA. BATHSHEBAH GREEN, b. c. 1775; d. after 1846.

1. Referred to as deceased in several Luzerne County, PA. deeds. No will or probate found, or place of burial.
2. According to family record of M. Farr, descendant of Francis. No further record of marriage date found.
3. Probably deceased because she is not mentioned in father's will. Her son John, however, is included.
4. Most dates are taken from the Phillips Family Bible.
5. Information per NSDAR Records.

6.

THE FAMILY OF EDWARD WILLIAMS

EDWARD WILLIAMS b. Wales, date unknown; d. date unknown. (1)
Married 1767
JEMIMAH WRIGHT b. date unknown; d. 179—

CHILDREN
Betsy b. 13 February, 1769
Edward b. 3 October, 1770
Polly b. 21 July, 1772 (twins)
John b. 21 July, 1772
John b. 6 July 1776
Tilly b. 6 March, 1778
Elijah b. December, 1779
Anson b. 16 October, 1781; d. 28 March, 1847 Orange Township, Delaware, Ohio. Buried in Williamsville Cemetery, Orange Township, Delaware, Ohio, m. 1st, Mary More, b. date unknown; d. 15 April 1811 [in childbirth]. 2nd, Hannah Phillips b. 1792, New York.; m. *c.* 1811, d. 12 August 1851, Orange Township, Delaware, Ohio. Buried in Williamsville Cemetery, Orange Township, Delaware, Ohio. (2)
Dolly b. 11 August, 1782
Rebecca b. 16 November, 1785
Robert b. 7 February 1788
James b. 20/22 May, 1790; d. 26 February, 1854 or 1864, possibly Wisconsin. m. Sarah Russell c.1810 b. 4 August 1795; d. 8 February, 1829 LeRoy, Genesee, NY.
Mary b. February, 179-
Artemeshe b. 1796; d. 1796

WILLIAMS, ANSON b. 16 October 1781; d. 28 March 1847, Orange Township, Delaware, Ohio, buried Williamsville Cemetery, Orange Twp., Delaware, Ohio, m. 1st, MARY MORE, h. date unknown; d. 15 April 1811 (in childbirth) probably N.Y. (3)

CHILDREN
Sarah/Sally [Calley] (4) b. 22 January 1806; d. 3 November, 1852, Orange Township, Delaware, Ohio, m. c. 1826, Isaac Bovee, b. unknown; d. unknown, Orange Township, Delaware, Ohio.
Jemimah b. 7 September, 1807
Jerrad Sanford b. 2 June, 1809; d. 18 September, 1848, Orange Township, Delaware, Ohio. m c. 1830, Catyann b. c 1810; d. 9 December, 1890, Orange Township, Delaware, Ohio.

m. 2nd, c. 1811, HANNAH PHILLIPS , b. 1792. New York; (5) d. 12 August 1851, Orange Township, Delaware, Ohio. Buried in Williamsville Cemetery, Orange Twp., Delaware, Ohio.
CHILDREN (6)
Mary (Polly in will) b. 8 June, 1812, d. 13 August, 1858, Orange Township, Delaware, Ohio, m. c. 1832, James Gibbs.
Anson b. 9 March, 1815; d. 9 March, 1815 prob. LeRoy, Genesee, NY.
Almira b. 7 September, 1817; d. 2 January, 1888, Orange Township, Delaware, Ohio, m. c. 1835/6, Ralph McCarty, b. c. 1812; d. 29 January, 1890, Orange Township, Delaware, Ohio.

Lucena b. 17 August, 1819; d. 5 April, 1837, Orange Township, Delaware, Ohio m. c. 1834; one child died in infancy.

Henry b. 12 September, 1820; d. 29 May, 1841, Orange Township, Delaware, Ohio.
John More b. 22 November, 1822/3; d. 28 July, 1899, buried Thomas Graveyard, Liberty Township, Delaware, Ohio, m 14 February, 1841, Annias Holcomb, b. c. 1823, d. probably after 1899.
Elizabeth b. 6 March, 1826 m. Mitchell Scoby.
Rebecca b. 20 June, 1830, LeRoy, Genesee, New York; (7) d. 17 February, 1857 (childbirth), Orange Township, Delaware, Ohio, m. 23 April, 1848, Delaware County, Ohio, Jerome B. Faulknor (8) b. c. 1822; d. 28 August, 1859, aged 26 y, 7 m, 27d. Buried Williamsville Cemetery, Orange Township, Delaware, Ohio.

JAMES WILLIAMS b. 20 May, 1790; d. 26 February 1854, maybe Winnecomme, Wisc. m. 1st, c. 1810, SARAH RUSSELL b. 4 August, 1795; d. 8 February 1829, LeRoy, Genesee, NY.

CHILDREN

Mary b. 11 August, 1811; d. 20 August, 1811.
Nancy b. 10 October, 1812; d. September, 1883. m. Lucius Thatcher.
Edward b. 29 October, 1814; d. April, 1899. Buried Plainville Cemetery (possibly Minnesota) m. 1st, Lucy Ann---- b. 1819; d. 13 May, 1852, (age 33 yrs) LeRoy, Genesee NY. Buried E. Main Cemetery, LeRoy, Genesee, NY; m 2nd, Emily J. Ely, 19 June, 1853, daughter of Enoch J and Lucretia T. Ely. b. 1830; d. 1 April, 1855 (age 25 yrs.) m. 3rd, Emma--
Cornell b. 11 August 1816
Jason b. 7 May, 1818; d. 15 February, 1884.
Marianna b. 30 June, 1820,; d. 18-14
Thomas b. 30 March, 1822; d. 15 December 1883
George b. 9 June, 1824
Judiann b. 23 April, 1826
Cordelia b. 3 September, 1827, d. 1899
Elijah b. 28 September, 1829, d. 1 March, 1899

m. 2nd, CORINTH A --- [d.-1831]
    No children

JOHN MORE b. 22 November, 1823; Genesee Co. NY, d. 28 July, 1899, Liberty Township, Delaware, Ohio, buried Thomas Graveyard, Liberty Twp, Delaware, Ohio. m. 14 February, 1841, ANNIAS HOLCOMB b. 9 April, 1824, CT. d. 29 November, 1910, Liberty Township, Delaware, Ohio. Buried Thomas Graveyard, Libert Twp, Delaware, Ohio. (9)

<u>Children</u> (10)
Henry A
Nancy E.
Rebecca A.
Cherry M.
Mary P.
Alvira D.
James H.
John

Solomon S.
Jennette
George
Mark

REBECCA WILLIAMS b. 20 June, 1830; LeRoy, Genesee, New York; (11) d. 17 February, 1857, (childbirth) Orange Township, Delaware, Ohio; buried Williamsville Cemetery, Orange Township, Delaware, Ohio. m. 23 April, 1848, Delaware County, Ohio,

JEROME B. FAULKNOR (12) b. c. 1822; d. 28 August, 1859. Aged 26 y, 7 m, 27d. Buried Williamsville Cemetery, Orange Township, Delaware, Ohio.

CHILDREN

    Sarah Francis. b. 1849; Orange Township, Delaware, Ohio, d. unknown; m. Reuben Poland, probably Orange Township, Delaware, Ohio. (13)
    Franklin (14)
    Jerome F. (15)
    Lewis   "

TOMBSTONE RECORDS - Delaware County, Ohio

WILLIAMSVILLE CEMETERY

Faulknor, Jerome B. d. Aug. 28, 1859, aged 37y 5m 26d
  Rebecca, his wife, d Feb. 17, 1857, aged 26y 7m 27d
  Solomon, son of J.B. & R., d Mar. 11; 1857, ae 1m 11d
  George W. son of J.B. & R., d Feb. 2, 1856, aged 9d
  Elizabeth M., dau. of J.B. & R., d Aug. 25, 1853 (or 5), aged 2y 8m 4d
  Mary A., dau. of J.B. & R., d Aug. 23, 1851, ae 10m 22ds
Williams, Fannie F., wife of R.B., 1866-1897
  Martha 1837-1923
  Cornelius S. 1842-1909
Williams, J.S. d Sept. 18, 1848, aged 39 y 1 m 28 d Father &
  Catyann d Dec. 9, 1890, aged 80y 7 m 14 d Mother
  Cornealia M, dau. of J.S. & Catyann d Dec. 30, 1847, ae 3y 9m 2d
Bovee, Sarah, wife of Isaac d Nov. 3, 1852, ae 46y 9 m 11d
Bovee, Isaac, d _____ (stone broken)
Williams, Henry A., Son of Anson & Hannah d May 29, 1841 ae 20y 9m 11d
Hannah, wife of A., d. Aug 12, 1851, ae 59Y
Anson, d Mar. 28, 1847, ae 6y 5m 12d
McCarty, Ralph, d. Jan. 29, 1890, ae 77y 7m 24d   Father &
Almire (16) d. Jan. 2, 1888, ae 70 y 3 m 27d   Mother
Gibbs, Mitchel, son of S.S & P. d. Nov. 8, 1841 ae 4y 9m 14d
Elizabeth, dau. of S.S & P. d. Dec. 25, 1841 ae 4m 17d
Rebecca, dau. of S.S & P. d. Nov. 16, 1848 ae 4 y 2m 16d

Mary, wife of S.S. (17) d. Aug. 13, 1858, aged 46y 2m 7d

REFERENCES

1. Birthdates from Williams' family bible. Copies made by F.W.R about 1940s. Handwritten pages headed "Florence Williams Line." In possession of Genesee Historical Society, Le Roy, NY. Note on record says, "copied from Bible taken by Anson Williams from New York State to Worthington, Ohio." Location of Original Bible unknown. Handwritten notation in same writing as rest of Bible notes says "The Williams family left LeRoy about 1850 and went to Wisconsin. All except Cornell [who] lived on farm, now Howells, at Lime Rock; early house was on 2nd Rd. E of LeRoy going South." The fact of all family members going to Wisconsin is incorrect. John Williams was in Delaware Co. Ohio and is shown on the 1820 census for that county in Sunbury. Anson Williams went to Delaware Co., Ohio in 1836 with his family. Anson purchased 1000 acres in the US Military Land section for $6,000. (Vol. 13, p. 234 and p. 255, Delaware Co. O). It may be that James Williams went to Wisconsin after the death of his first wife. This line has not been researched.

2. There is a separate page headed <u>Anson Williams</u> (From Family Bible (FWR). A notation says "Anson Williams was Tavern Keeper who moved from Cherry Valley to Delaware Co., Ohio taking with him about 30 people including daughters with husbands (Abraham Louke, James Gibson [should be Gibbs], Ralph McCarty, Mitchell Scoby -in Ohio records, he is Seaby) and sons with wives. Founded Williamsville, Ohio. A notation in a different handwriting says "was a Tavernkeeper in Cherry Valley N.Y. He was the original owner of 4 farms in LeRoy."

3. Anson Williams is shown as a purchaser on October 17, 1809 in Archives of Holland Land Company; Reel# 487, pg. 56 and Reel #495, pg. 93. Filmed State University College at Fredonia, NY. Probably children of first marriage born in NY State.

4. In Bible, name is Calley. In the will of Anson Williams, refers to his daughter Sally; on tombstone shown as Sarah.

5. *History of Delaware County and* Ohio, page 677, says Hannah was from Pennsylvania. The 1850 Orange, Ohio census states that she was born in New York.

6. A series of Deeds starting 11 February, 1815 shows Anson and Hannah "of LeRoy", Genesee, NY. They resided there until 1836, when they removed to Ohio. All children of this marriage probably born in LeRoy, Genesee, NY. On the 1830 Genesee Co. New York census, Anson is shown with a household of 2 m twenty to thirty, 1 m fifteen to twenty, 1 m ten to fifteen, 2 m five to ten, 1 m under five; 2 f twenty to thirty, 1 f fifteen to twenty, 2 f ten to fifteen, 2 f under 5. Probably 1 m twenty

to thirty is Isaac Bovee, Sarah's husband.

7. Anson Williams, in will dated April, 1847 leaves Rebecca Williams his house and several town lots, also 20 acres of land. He specifies that she is to take care of her mother Hannah, who in 1850 is living with Rebecca, her husband Jerome Faulkner and daughter Sarah. (Delaware, Ohio 1850 census), He leaves his "grandson Henry C." a house and two town lots. His son Jared S is mentioned and his daughters Polly Gibbs, Almira McCarty, Elizabeth Seaby, Sally Bovee. Also includes grandsons George and Cornelius Williams. (George, son of John M. Williams.) Jemima is not included, probably deceased by then.

8. Marriage listed in *Delaware County Marriage Records;* "married by Solomon Dunton." Notation next to marriage date says "Gazette", possibly referring to a newspaper marriage announcement. Record at Delaware County Historical Society, Delaware, Ohio.

9. John More Williams came to Orange Township (Williamsville) with his parents. After their death, he and his wife and family resided on the family estate until about 1859, when they moved lo Liberty Township, where he resided until his death in 1899. He is buried in the Thomas Graveyard in Liberty Twp. With his wife Annis Holcomb.

10. Children listed in *History of Delaware County and Ohio,* page 677. On the 1850 census, the following children are shown: Henry, 8years old; Nancy E., 7 years old; Almera R, 4 years old; Cherry M, 2 years old; Mary P, 7 months old.

11. There are two probate files on record in Delaware County; file #806, a guardianship containing 61 pages which deals with the property the surviving children of Rebecca Faulknor inherited from her. This case was not completed until 1866 or 1867.

12. Case # 917 is the estate of Jerome Faulkner who left one child by his second wife Marietta McCarty.

13. Sarah and Reuben Poland moved to Union County, Ohio shortly after their marriage.

14. Name taken from document of sale of real estate. May 31, 1858 found with probate records.

15. Names from notice of Guardian Sale in Delaware Gazette, commencing December 22, 1866 found with probate records. There may have been other children not listed.

16. Name spelled with an "e" on tombstone; with an "a" in Bible.

17. This is thought to be the wife of James Gibb and daughter of Anson and Hannah Williams.

CHAPTER IX
Will of Henry Lott, Deceased
DELAWARE COUNTY OHIO WILL BOOK
VOL II, Pages 267-9

Pleas held at the Court House of Delaware on the 24th day of July AD 1844 before the Honorable Joseph R. Swan President and Ahab Jinks, Marshall L. Griffin and William G. Norris Esq. his Associate Judges of the Court of Common Pleas in and 'for the County of Delaware in the State of Ohio.

This day the last will and testament of Henry Lott dec'd was produced in open Court and proved by the testimony of the subscribing witnesses thereto, as reduced to writing approved and ordered to be recorded and whereupon on motion Mary Lott, widow of said Henry Lott deceased appeared in open court and made her election to take under said will. And on motion of Oliver Stark one of the Executors in said will named Mary Lott the other Executor named having declined acting as per file. It is ordered that letters ... be granted the said Oliver Stark upon his entering into bonds in the sum of $360.00 with Isaac Finch and Sidney Moon as security. And it is further ordered that Cornelius Richards, James Stark and Joseph Patrick appraise the personal property of said Estate and also if required said appraisers to appraise the real estate.

I, Henry Lott of the County of Delaware in the State of Ohio do make and publish this my last will and testament in manner and form following that is lo say. First it is my will that my funeral expenses and all my just debts be fully paid.

2nd I give devise and bequeath to my beloved wife Mary Lott the plantation on which we now reside situated in Kingston Township, Delaware County & State aforesaid supposed to be fifty acres of land, my will is that my wife Mary have the foregoing described farm to have to dispose of the same as she thinks right and proper, also all the live stock, cattle, sheep and hogs by me now owned &... thereon also all the household furniture and other items not particularly named and otherwise disposed of in this will, she however disposing of as much thereof to pay my just debts as aforesaid.

And lastly I hereby constitute and appoint my said wife Mary Lott and Oliver Stark to be Executors for this my last will and testament revoking and annulling all former wills by me made and ratifying and confirming this and no other to be my last will and testament. In testimony whereof I have hereunto set my hand and seal the 20th day of April AD 1844. Signed published and declared by the above named Henry Lott as & for his last will and testament. In presence of us who at his request have signed as witness to the same.
Isaac Finch, Jacob C. Rosencrans   Henry Lott [Seal]

The State of Ohio Delaware County

Court of Common Pleas July Term 1844, Personally appeared in open Court Isaac Finch and Jacob Rosencrans who being duly sworn depose & say that the paper before them purporting to be the last will & testament of Henry Lott now deceased was by the said Henry Lott acknowledged published & declared to be his last will & testament in the presence of these depondents, that the said deceased was of lawful age that he was of sound disposing mind & memory, & under no restraint as they duly believe that they subscribe the same as witnesses in the presence & at the request of the testator & in the presence of each other

                        Isaac Finch, Jacob Rosencrans his mark
                                                            X

Sworn to & subscribed in open Court this 23rd day of July AD 1844

Recorded the foregoing will on August 3rd 1844

                                          Attest   WD Heins Clark

I hereby decline acting as one of the Executors of the last will and testament of my deceased husband and wish Mr. Stark to act as sole executor.

July 23, 1844   Mary Lott

I hereby declare writing as one of the executors of the last will and testament of my deceased husband I wish he Stark to visit his late Essington

July 23 1844 Mary Latt

Inventory

Schedule of the Goods and Chattles belonging to the estate of Henry Lot [mispelled] to which the widow is entitled without being obliged to account for the same.

Wearing apparal of Dec'd
2 Spinning wheels
1 Loom
2 Bibles
6 Other Books
1 Red Fan
2 Sheets
Wool Yarn and Cloth Flax
4 Bedsteads Beds and Be[d]ding
1 Table
6 Chairs
6 Knives and Forks
6 Plates Teacups and Sau[ce]rs
1 Milkpot
1 Teapot
1 Spoon
Given under our hands this Day and Year aforesaid
        Joseph Patrick Cornelius Richards - Appraisers
        James Stark

State of Ohio Delaware County SS

 Before me Oliver Stark a Justice of the Peace in and for said County personally came Joseph Patrick, Cornelius Richards and James Stark, appraisers of the Estate of Henry Lott late of Kingston Township in said County Del. and were sworn well and truly to appraise all the Goods and Chattles of said Estate which shall be presented to them for appraisement and also to set off to the widow of said deceas[ed) such provision or other property as they shall think reasonably for the support of herself and child for twelve months.
Given under my hand this 5th day of August 1844
        Oliver Stark JP

 We further state that we have set off to widow and one child the sum of two hundred and twenty five dollars for one year support. She has taken all the personal property at the appraisal amounting to one hundred and forty nine dollars and 49 cents. Given under our hands on the Day and Year aforesaid.
        Joseph Patrick Cornelius Richards - Appraisers
        James Stark

 We further certify that according to the order of the Court we have viewed and appraised a p[iece] of Land belonging to the aforesaid Estate taken off of the South East Corner of said Farm supposed to be twelve acres. We do appraise said Land at fifteen dollars per acre.
Given under our hands this 5th Day of August 1844.
        Joseph Patrick Cornelius Richards - Appraisers
        James Stark

Attest

Oliver Stark

True and accurate Inventory of the Goods and Chattles of Henry Lott of the Township of Kingston in the County of Delaware Ohio as presents to the undersigned Joseph Patrick, Cornelius Richards and James Stark appraisers appointed by the Court of Common Pleas of said County by Oliver Stark Executor of said Estate this 5th Day of August AD 1844.

1 Cupboard and Dishes	$2.50
1 Churn	.62
1 Shovel & Tongs	.75
1 Clock	1.00
1 Looking Glass	.50
1 Ax	.50
2 Iron Kettles	4.00
3 Trunks	1.00
1 Beattle and Wig	1.00
1 Chair	.50
1 Yoke of Oxen	45.00
1 Black Cow	7.00
1 White Faced Cow	8.00
1 Heifer	5.00
1 Tub of Pot[atoes]	10.00
1 Tub of Corn	8.50
1 Staple and Ring	.50
1 Fanning Mill	7.00
1 Mow of Wheat	15.00
2 Tons of Hay	6.00
3 Calves	3.00
7 Boards	.50
2 Barrels	.75
6 Hogs	6.00
20 Gees[e]	2.50
1 Fro (?)	.37 1/2
2 Cows	12.00
Total Amount of Appraisal	$149.49

The State of Ohio, Delaware County, ss:

Be it remembered, that on this 10th day of September A.D. 1844 personally appeared Oliver Stark Executor- on the Estate of Henry Lott deceased, and makes oath that the inventory by him signed, and hereunto annexed, is in all respects just and true:

That it contains a true statement of all the estate and property of the said deceased, which has come to the knowledge of such Executor and particularly of all money, bank bills, or other circulating medium belonging to the said deceased, and of the said deceased against such Executor or other persons, according to the best of his knowledge. Oliver Stark

Subscribed and sworn to me the date aforesaid, W.D. Heins Clerk Del. Com. Pleas

MARY LOTT'S WILL
DELAWARE COUNTY, OHIO RECORDS OF WILLS
Vol. 11, Pages 331-2

Proceeding at the Court House in the town of Delaware County, Ohio, before his honor Ezias Bowen President of the sixth judicial Circuit of Ohio, and William G. Norris, Marshal S. Griffin and Aluron Stark, his associate judges of the Court of Common Pleas for the County aforesaid in the thirtieth day of September AD, one thousand eight hundred and forty six, Be it remembered that at the time and place aforesaid during the session of the September term of the Court of Common Pleas aforesaid the Last Will and Testament of Mary Lott deceased was produced in open Court and proven by the oath of Reuben C. Gardner and Samuel W. Trumbull the subscribing witnesses thereto and ordered to be recorded, which said will and the testimony of said witnesses is of the words and figures following to wit;

I bequeath to Robert Wells 14 acres of land on which I now reside, lying in Kingston Township, Delaware County and State of Ohio. The said Robert Wells being privileged to bequeath the said land to whom he sees fit after my decease.

I bequeath to Isaac Dayton Taner 10 acres of land belonging to the said farm in the said Tp. Co. and State. The said Isaac Dayton Taner being privileged to bequeath the said 10 acres of land to whom he shall see fit after my decease. The above mentioned parties shall make such a division of the farms as they can agree upon between themselves.

Likewise the aforesaid Robert Wells and Isaac Dayton Taner shall see that my brother Thomas Simmons shall be taken good care of as long as he lives provided he shall outlive me. And if the said parties neglect to observe and do as I have willed concerning the said Thomas Simmons, but shall leave him in want, then shall they forfeit the whole of the above mentioned land and it shall be conferred upon any person who shall take and provide for him during his life.

I bequeath to the said parties and equal division of all the loose property which may be left after defraying all debts and funeral expenses.

The above mentioned parties shall pay or cause to be paid the sum of 20 dollars to Henry Lott Trumbull.

The said parties see that all my bisness is settled and all debts paid without other administrators. This is my last Will and Testament given this 15th day of May AD 1845 wherewith I set my hand and Seal in the presence of
                                                          Mary Lott [Seal]
R.C. Gardner
Samuel Trumbull

The State of Ohio, Delaware County in Court of Common Pleas September Term 1846. Personally appeared in open court R.C.Gardner and Samuel W. Trumbull who being duly sworn depose and say that the paper before them purporting to be the last Will and Testament of Mary Lott now deceased was by the said Mary Lott acknowledged, published and declared to be her last Will and Testament in the presence of these deposed that the said deceased was of lawful age, that she was of sound and disposing mind, and under no restraint as they verily believe that they subscribed the same as witnesses in the presence and at the request of the Testator and in presence of each other . Reuben C. Gardner Samuel W. Trumbull. Sworn to and subscribed in open court this 30th day of Sept. AD 1846   Wm. D. Heiser Clark

ANSON WILLIAMS WILL
DELAWARE COUNTY WILLS
Vol. 2, P. 347-9

The State of Ohio Delaware County

Proceedings before the Honorable Wm G Norris, Marshal S Griffin and Alicon Stark Associate Judges of the Court of Common Pleas for said County on the seventeenth day of April AD 1847.

This day the Last Will & Testament of Anson Williams Dec. was produced in open Court and duly proven by the oaths of Aloa MacOmber and Samuel McCritcheon the subscribing witness thereto whose testimony was reduced to writing. And it appearing to the Court that the deceased at the time of executing said will was of sound mind memory and understanding and under no restraint. It is therefore ordered that said Will and the Testimony so taken be entered of record.

Will

I Anson Williams of the County of Delaware in the State of Ohio, make and publish this my last Will and Testament in manner and form following that is to say;

1st. It is my will that my funeral expenses and all my just debts be fully paid

2nd I give devise and bequeath to my daughter Rebecca my dwelling house and outbuildings on the west side of the Columbus and Sandusky Turnpike Road and also six town lots viz. to commence at Von Zaron street and thence running north along the Columbus and Sandusky road to take three front lots and three back lots immediately west of the three first described. Also twenty acres of land commencing at the South east corner of JS Williams land thence west along said line far enough to contain twenty acres by following at the center of the Mathews brook opposite of the Olentangs street. Also twenty acres of land to commence at the southwest corner of lands owned by Jos Fuller thence south along the sections line to land sold to Lorenzo and Augustus Thomas, thence forty rods along said line, thence to strike the Mathew brook and thence to follow said brook far enough east by running a line due north to contain twenty acres by running west to the place of beginning and the privilage of a road on the South lines of JS Williams and Jos Fullers lines so as to get to the said west twenty acres and if the said Rebecca Williams should die and leave no heirs then the above described property is to be divided by my Executors. Also all the household furniture. And my wife Hannah is to live with the said Rebecca and the said Rebecca is to clothe and maintain her mother together with the assistance of my Executors during her natural life, this in lieu of her dower.

3rd I give and divise to my two grandsons George and Cornelius Williams ten acres of land bounded north by JS Williams and D Trellins lands west by lands willed lo Rebecca Williams, south to the center of the Mathews brook, up said brook far enough by a north line to the place of beginning to make ten acres.

4th I give and devise to my son Jared S Williams all the lands more or less that lies between George and Cornelius land on the last and as far south as the said Mathews brook and north to the line or road that is to be for the use of the said Rebecca.

5th I give and devise to my grandson Henry C Williams a house and two town lots that the house stands on, on the east side of the Columbus and Sandusky Turnpike road and seven acres of land which I own on the west side of Washington street and bounded north by John M Williams land and east to the center of the said Johns land and south to GS Salsbury lands.

6th. I do further request that if my son John M Williams shall stand in need of any assistance for my Executors to do it.

7th I give and devise to my 4 daughters Sally Bovee, Polly Gibbs, Almira McCarty, Elizabeth Seaby, fifty dollars cash to be paid to them in clothing by my executors when they have funds in their hands, not for other purposes.

8th I do further request that Samuel McCutchison is to have the privileges that he now has so long as he shall want by paying the interest and tax for the premises that he now occupies. Also I request that my son JS Williams to have the privil[e]ge of putting in two horses in the stable which I have willed to my daughter Rebecca for a reasonable time and lastly I hereby constitute and appoint Collins P Ellibro and Samuel McCutchison to be the Executors of this my last Will and Testament, revoking and annulling all former Wills……..that my Executors have the power to dispose of all my property which is not herein disposed both real and personal and further I declare the article of agreement to be valid between me and Joel Galland for the time therin named and satisfying and confirming this and no other to be my last Will and Testament. In testimony whereof I have set my hand and seal this twenty second day of February AD 1847.

Signed, sealed, published and declared by the above so named Anson Williams as and for his last Will and Testament in person of us who at his request have signed as witnesses to the same.   Anson [Seal] Williams

            Alva Macomb   Samuel McCutchison

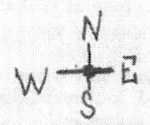

The Williamsville Cemetery
Orange Township, Delaware Co., Ohio

BIBLIOGRAPHY

Archives of the Holland Land Company, S.U.N.Y., Fredonia, New York.

Brown, Hildah Phillips. Private Papers. Lackawanna Historical Society, Scranton Pennsylvania.

DAR, The Official Roster of the Soldiers of The American Revolution Buried in the State of Ohio. n.d.

DAR Official Roster Ill. Soldiers of the Revolution Who Lived in the State of Ohio. 1959.

DAR, Marriage Records, Delaware County, Ohio, 1832-1865, 3 Vols.

DAR Patriot Index.

Delaware County Ohio Deed Book, Vol. 4.

Delaware County Ohio Deed Book, Vol. 8.

Delaware County Ohio Deed Book, Vol. 13.

Delaware County Ohio Deed Book, Vol. 29.

Delaware County Ohio Deed Book, Vol. 31.

Delaware County Ohio Probate Records.

Delaware County Ohio Will Book, Vol. 2.

Delaware Gazette.

Everts, L.H. Illustrated Historical Atlas of Delaware County, 1875.

Family Bible, John Phillips.

Family Bible, Edward Williams. Genesee County, New York, Minutes; Court of Common Pleas, 1820- 1827.

Genesee County, New York Deed Books.

History of Delaware County and Ohio, Chicago, O.L. Baskin & Co. 1880, Reprint 1975.

International Genealogical Index.

Knepper, George W. Ohio and Its People, Kent, Ohio and London, England. The Kent University Press. 1989.

List of Male Inhabitants in Delaware County, Ohio, 1835. Luzerne County Pennsylvania Deeds, Vol. 1-10.

Luzerne County Pennsylvania Orphan's Court Docket; Vol. 1.

Lytle, James R., Twentieth Century History of Delaware County Ohio, 1908.

Mapes, Dianna Miller, Guy E. Mapes. Burials in Sunbury Memorial Park; Sunbury, Delaware, Ohio, published privately, 1991.

Obituary, John Phillips, <u>Wilkes-Barre Advocate</u>.

Pierce, Stewart. Annals of Luzerne County, Philadelphia: J.B Lippincott &Co.1866.

Plat of Williamsville, Delaware County, Ohio Plat Book, Book Two.

Powell, Esther Weygandt. Tombstone Inscriptions and Other Records of Delaware County, Ohio, Published Privately, 1972.

Probate Records, W. Greenwich, Rhode Island.

Proceedings and Collections of the Wyoming Historical and Geological Society, Vol. IV. Wilkes-Barre, Pennsylvania, 1899.

Revolutionary War Pension, John Phillips, # S. 7308.

Revolutionary War Pension, Zephaniah Lott, # R. 6458.

Rhode Island Vital Records, E. Greenwich, Rhode Island.

Rhode Island Vital Records, W. Greenwich, Rhode Island.

U.S. Census, Delaware County, Ohio, 1820.

U.S. Census, Delaware County, Ohio, 1830.

U.S. Census, Delaware County, Ohio, 1840.

U.S. Census, Delaware County, Ohio, 1850.

U.S. Census, Genesee County, New York, 1830.

U.S. Census, Luzerne County, Pennsylvania, 1790.

U.S. Census, Luzerne County, Pennsylvania, 1800.

U.S. Census, Luzerne County, Pennsylvania, 1810.

War of 1812 Pension, Joseph Lott, Survivor Certificate #24305.

Will, Arthur Aylesworth. Rhode Island Probate Records.

Williams Family File, LeRoy House. LeRoy, Genesee, New York.

Wyoming County, Pennsylvania Deed Book, Vol. 19.

INDEX

Abington Baptist church 48
Abington, Pennsylvania xx, 24
Allegheny 86
Anways, Mr. 115
Atherton, Rufus 77
Aylesworth family xx
Aylesworth, Demis xviii
Aylesworth, Arthur xviii
Baptist preacher 95
Bartley, Widow 62
Bates, Hitty 43
Bates, Joshua 43, 56
Bates, Sabra 110
Battle of Kittaning, Pennsylvania xx
Beekman, New York xx
Bennington, Ohio 62, 87, 114
Blanchard, Jeremiah 99
Bovee, Isaac 102
Bovee, Sally 139
Bovee, Sarah 102
Brittain, James 90
Brown, Hildah Phillips xii, xv, 92
Brown, James 114
Brown, Sarah 63
Brown, Silence 114
Bucks County militia xx
Bucks County, Pennsylvania xx
Budd, John 99
Buffalo, New York 24, 53, 80
Carey, Jabez 43, 57
Carey, Mother 73
Carey, Silas 58, 61, 65, 73, 76, 78, 84, 88, 95, 101, 104, 117
Carmel, New York xx
Carney, Sarah (Sally) 25, 29, 51
Carpenter, Hewitt Betsy 43, 69, 73, 87, 91, 114
Carpenter, Gilbert xviii, xix, 29
Cartherton, Robert 73
Chamberlain, Mary xiii, xx
Cherry Valley, New York xxi
Clark, Aurora 64, 70, 76, 103, 110, 114, 115, 117
Clark, Nancy 64, 70, 76, 103, 110, 114, 115, 117
Clark, Sally Tripp 57, 59, 61, 63, 64
Clark, Silas 59, 64, 73, 76, 84, 103
Cleveland, Ohio 80
Columbus, Ohio xvi, 66
Connecticut Land Company xix, xx
Cough syrup recipe 50
Delaware County Historical Society xv
Delaware County Ohio xiii, xvi, xxi, xxii, 24
Delaware County, History of xvi
Delaware, Ohio xv
Doud, Deborah (see Phillips)
Dunkins Plains, Ohio 99
Dutchess County, New York xx
Dyer, Mr. 115
E. Greenwich, Rhode Island xviii
East Liberty, Ohio 99
Elhbro, Collins 139
Family Bible, Phillips 24
Felts, Polly 52, 60, 67, 70, 79, 103, 110

Finch, Daniel 56
Finch, Isaac 56, 132
First Baptist Church xx
Flax 34, 35, 39, 42, 68, 72, 109
Franklin county xvi
Franklinton xvi
Fuller, Joseph 138
Galland, Joel 139
Gardner, Reuben 137
Gautier, Stephen 30, 78, 104, 107
Genesee County, New York xiii, xix, xxi, xxii, 25, 28
Gibbs, Polly 139
Giles, Mr. 24
Goodrich, George 67
Goodrich, Mary Phillips 95
Goodrich, Mr. 110
Green, Bathshebah xx, 115
Greglery, James 110
Grist, Mr.& Mrs. 34
Grist, Rachel 63
Harding, Lydia Tripp (see Phillips)
Hewitt, Isaac 26, 59, 63, 67, 110
Hewitt, Lavina (see Russell)
Hewitt, Mary 26, 31, 43, 60
Hewitt, Mary Phillips 63, 88, 106
Hillman, Mrs., death of 99
Holland Land Company xxii
Huff, Mr. 34
Hutchings, Betsy 99
Hutchings, William 99
Inventory, Lott property 135
Ithaca, New York 56
Jenkins, John 88
John Ross 109

Johnstown, Ohio 79
Kimble family 84, 102, 109, 114
Kimble, Mr. 87, 91, 93, 98, 111
Kimble, Mrs. 94, 98, 106, 111, 117
Kingston. Pennsylvania 24, 51
Kingston Township, Delaware County, Ohio xvi, 137
Lackawanna xiii
Lackawanna Historical Society, xii, xix, xv
Le Roy House, xv
Lee, George 98, 101
Lee, Tryphena Hewitt 74, 82, 95, 96, 101,114
LeRoy Historical Society xv
LeRoy, New York xv, xix, xxii, 46
Liberty Township, Ohio xxii
Lott's route to Kingston, Ohio 24
Lott, Elizabeth 81
Lott, Elsann 106
Lott, Else 24, 25, 34, 43, 48, 51, 54, 58, 63, 65, 72, 75, 77, 88, 91
Lott, Else, birthday 65
Lott, Else, death of 93
Lott, Henderick xxi
Lott, Henry xx, 24, 25, 28, 30, 34, 35, 36, 37, 38, 43, 46, 47, 51, 52, 55, 56, 61, 62, 67, 72, 73, 74, 75, 80, 86, 90, 91, 94, 96, 107, 109, 110, 115, 116, 117, 135, 136
Lott, Henry, inventory 136
Lott, Henry, uncle of xxi
Lott, Henry, will 132

Lott, Isaac 62
Lott, Joseph 29, 65, 96
Lott, Leonard 25, 29, 34, 58, 98, 99, 101, 104, 105, 113
Lott, Leonard, daughter of 68
Lott, Mary xii, xiii, xiv, xv, xvi, xviii, xix, xxi, xxii, 29, 67, 132, 133, 137
Lott, Mary, birthday 92
Lott, Samantha 29, 59, 62, 67, 75, 78, 82, 83, 88, 91, 93, 94, 96, 98, 102, 106, 114
Lott, Sarah (Sally) (see Carney)
Lott, Stephen 56, 62
Lott, Zephaniah xxi, 24, 25, 28
Lott, Zephaniah, death of 34
Luzerne County Pennsylvania xiii, xviii, xix, xxi
Luzerne County, Pennsylvania Orphan's Court, 29
MacComb Alva 138
Making Linen Fabric 39
Making Wool Fabric 40
Marcy, John xix
McCarty, Almira 139
McCuthison, Samuel 138, 139
Mehoopany, Pennsylvania xxi
Methodist church xvi
Methodist schoolhouse 95
Middlebury, Genesee Co. New York 104
Millard, Polly Tripp 59, 70, 76, 88, 95
Millard, Solomon 83, 90, 95, 98, 106
Millard, Thomas 85
Miller, Caleb 103
Miller, Elder John 49, 73, 115
Miller, John 70

Miller, Lois 52, 110
Miller, Louis 110
Miller, Mary Goodrich 67, 70
Miller, Melissa (see Schwartz)
Miller, Samuel xiii, 43, 70, 79, 103
Miller, Stephen xiii, 63, 67, 70, 103, 110, 114, 115, 117
Miller, Susannah xiii, 79, 103, 110, 114, 115, 117
Montrose, Pennsylvania 42
Moon, Sidney 132
Mullenix, Pennelia 95
New England xvi
New Jersey, xvi
New York State xxi, 25, 30, 43, 56
New York, xvi
Newark, Ohio 80
Trumbull, Harriet 76
Number of letters xii
Ohio xvi, xix, xxi, xxii
Old Northwest Territory xvi
Orange Township, Ohio xxii
Osburn, James 65
Parker, Amanda Miller 43, 64, 65, 70, 73, 76, 84, 103, 114
Parker, Lorenzo 67
Patrick, Joseph 132, 135, 136
Pennsylvania xii, xvi, xx, xxi
Phillips family Bible xii, xviii
Phillips, Comer 43, 70, 79, 95, 103, 115, 117
Phillips, Cornwell xix, xviii, 26, 33, 34, 35, 36, 37, 38, 42, 49, 54, 59, 63, 65, 69, 72, 75, 78, 81, 104, 107, 111, 113, 114, 117
Phillips, Deborah Dowd 26, 81

Phillips, DeWitt 110
Phillips, Esther 35, 38
Phillips, Fanny 79, 84, 88
Phillips, Francis xviii, xix, xx, 76, 95, 99, 104, 107
Phillips, Francis II xix
Phillips, Hannah (see Williams)
Phillips, Hannah Mott 43
Phillips, Hosea 104, 117
Phillips, John xii, xiii, xviii, xix, xx, 24, 26, 49, 107, 115
Phillips, John, daughters xx
Phillips, John, pension xix
Phillips, Lovisa 104
Phillips, Lydia 42, 47, 49, 50, 61, 67, 68, 73, 79, 82, 90, 95, 96, 100, 101, 104, 114, 115
Phillips, Mary (see Lott)
Phillips, Polly 43
Phillips, Zacheous xix, 104
Phillips, Mary (see Hewitt)
Phillips, Thomas (see Simmons)
Porter Cemetery xxi
Portland, Ohio (see Sandusky)
Pownal, Bennington County, Vermont xx
Presbyterians 108
Price of goods 86
Protracted meeting 108
Purdy, Lois 95, 107
Purdy, Mary 101
Purdy, Tryphena 98
Purdy, Mary 103
Reformed Netherlands Dutch Church, xx
Revivals, religious 25
Richards, Cornelius 110, 132, 135, 136

Richard Nathaniel 110
Richards, Peter 110
Rosencranse, Abraham 29, 30, 34, 48, 102, 103
Rosencranse, Daniel 26, 29, 30, 48, 54, 58, 75
Rosencranse, Isaac 34
Rosencranse, Isaac, Mrs., Death of 34
Rosencranse, Josiah 58
Rosencranse, Mrs. 30
Rosecrans, William Stark xvi
Ross, James 62, 68, 69, 72, 77, 84, 85, 86, 88, 90, 93, 99, 104, 110
Ross, James, wife of 94
Ross, John 82, 90, 94
Ross, Mr. 65, 69, 87, 94, 99, 102, 109, 110, 114, 117
Ross, Mr. and Mrs. 66
Ross, Mrs. 114
Ross, Nancy 90
Ross, Nathan 102
Ros Samuel 78, 79, 117
Ross, Ziba 77
Russell, Albert 66, 67, 117
Russell, John 38, 42, 49, 52, 55, 59, 66, 67, 69, 72, 74, 87, 91, 96, 104, 109, 110, 114
Russell, Lavina Hewitt 26, 31, 42, 49, 52, 55, 59, 67, 69, 72, 74, 91, 96, 104, 110, 114
Russell, Lavina Sarah 67
Russell, Louis 66
Russell, Mary Aurora 67
Russell, Polly 66
Russell, Retha 114
Russell, Sarah 66
Russell, Thomas 65, 66, 72, 73, 74, 78, 79, 82, 87, 91, 95,

98, 100, 101, 102, 107, 113, 115, 116, 117
Sandusky County, Ohio xxii
Sandusky, Erie County, Ohio xvi, 24, 53
Schwartz, Melissa 38
Scranton, Pennsylvania. xii, xv
Seaby, Elizabeth 139
Silsbee, David 59, 62, 75, 78, 82, 83, 88, 91, 93, 96, 98, 111, 113, 116
Simmons, Thomas 24, 28, 30, 33, 37, 44, 48, 51, 53, 55, 56, 59, 72, 73, 74, 75, 76, 77, 79, 81, 85, 90, 95, 96, 100, 104, 109, 113, 114, 115, 116, 137
Tripp, David 107
Slavery 108
Smith, John 58
Smith, Rachel 58
Stafford, New York xxi, 25
Stark, Betsy 83, 104
Stark, James xxii, 83, 132, 135, 136
Stark, Oliver 132, 135
Stephens, Peter 51
Sufferers xix, 107
Sugar camp 46, 47
Sugaring 47, 58, 72
Sunbury Post Office, Ohio 24
Sunbury, Ohio 43, 57, 63
Tanner, Isaac Dayton xxii, 115, 116, 117, 137
Taylor, Jedidiah 72
Taylor, Preserved 110
Tayner, Isaac Dayton (see Tanner)
Thomas, Augustus 138
Thomas, Lorenzo 138

Trellins, D. 138
Tripp, David 85, 90, 106
Tripp, David, Mrs. 88
Tripp, James 36, 49, 70, 85, 90, 95, 98,115
Tripp, James, Mrs. 88
Tripp, Permelia 113
Trumbull, Harriet 26, 57, 65, 69, 73, 79, 81, 104
Trumbull, Mr. 62, 117
Tunkhannock, Pennsylvania 56
U.S. Military District xvi
Van Buren, President 111
Van Pelt, Else (see Lott)
W. Greenwich, Rhode Island xviii
Wells, Harriet 54
Wells, Robert xxii, 26, 54, 55, 59, 65, 69, 71, 73, 76, 79, 81, 98, 104, 115, 116, 137
Wesleyan University xvi
Westmoreland County, State of Connecticut, xix
Wheeler, Anna 102, 109, 111
Wheeler, Anny 98, 106, 113, 116
White, Eber 67
White, Mercy 67
Wilcox, Gardener 58, 61
Wilcox, Gilbert 58
Wilcox, Jane 58
Wilcox, Mr. 83
Wilcox, Thankful 26
Wilcox, Jane 61
Wilkes-Barre, Pennsylvania 51
Williams family Bible. xv, xxi
Williams Sally Russell 46
Williams, Anson xix, xxi, xxii,

28, 30, 38, 49, 53, 54, 59, 65, 69, 72, 75, 78, 80, 81, 85, 87, 90, 97, 102, 104, 107, 111, 117, 138
Williams, Anson, will 138
Williams, Cornelius 138
Williams, Edward xxi
Williams, Elizabeth 97
Williams, Esther 88
Williams, George 138
Williams, Hannah xxii, 26, 52, 65, 79, 80, 87, 90, 94 97, 98, 102, 111, 138
Williams, Henry C. 138
Williams, James 46, 52, 54
Williams, Jared 5. 138
Williams, Jemimah xxi •
Williams, Jerrad Sanford xxi
Williams, John xxii, 47, 63, 80, 90, 98
Williams, John More xxii, 139
Williams, John Mr. 59, 63, 88, 91
Williams, John, death of 93
Williams, Lucena, death of 97
Williams, Nancy 52, 54
Williams, Rebecca 80, 97, 138, 139
Williams, Sanford 90
Williams, Calley (Sally) xxi
Williams, Rebecca xxii
Williamsville Cemetery xxii
Williamsville, Ohio xxii
Wilson, Amzi 30, 78, 85, 103
Wilson, John 104
Wilson, Merritt 30, 104, 107
Wilson, Phelena Wetherby 57
Wilson, Phelena Wetherby, death of 85
Wilson, Sarah 104

Wright, Jemimah xxi
Wyoming County, Pennsylvania xxi, xiii
Wyoming Valley, Pennsylvania, xix
Zoar, Delaware, Ohio 43

Made in the USA
Columbia, SC
14 May 2025